Activities for the
Differentiated
Classroom

Gayle H. Gregory • Carolyn Chapman

CORWIN PRESS
Classroom

For information:

Corwin Press
A SAGE Publications Company
2455 Teller Road
Thousand Oaks, California 91320
CorwinPress.com

SAGE, Ltd.
1 Oliver's Yard
55 City Road
London EC1Y 1SP
United Kingdom

SAGE India Pvt. Ltd.
B 1/I 1 Mohan Cooperative
Industrial Area
Mathura Road, New Delhi
India 110 044

SAGE Asia-Pacific Pvt. Ltd.
33 Pekin Street #02-01
Far East Square
Singapore 048763

Printed in the United States of America.

ISBN 978-1-4129-5341-2

This book is printed on acid-free paper.

08 09 10 11 12 10 9 8 7 6 5 4 3 2 1

Executive Editor: Kathleen Hex
Managing Developmental Editor: Christine Hood
Editorial Assistant: Anne O'Dell
Developmental Writer: Sally Griffith
Proofreader: Bette Darwin
Art Director: Anthony D. Paular
Cover Designer: Monique Hahn
Interior Production Artist: Lisa Riley

Activities *for the* Differentiated Classroom

GRADE **5**

TABLE OF CONTENTS

Connections to Standards

This chart shows the national academic standards that are covered in each chapter.

MATHEMATICS	Standards are covered on pages
Numbers and Operations—Understand numbers, ways of representing numbers, relationships among numbers, and number systems.	16, 20
Numbers and Operations—Compute fluently, and make reasonable estimates.	14, 17
Algebra—Understand patterns, relations, and functions.	10
Geometry—Analyze characteristics and properties of two-and three-dimensional shapes, and develop mathematical arguments about geometric relationships.	15
Data Analysis and Probability—Formulate questions that can be addressed with data, and collect, organize, and display relevant data to answer them.	9
Data Analysis and Probability—Select and use appropriate statistical methods to analyze data.	11
Problem Solving—Apply and adapt a variety of appropriate strategies to solve problems.	12

SCIENCE	Standards are covered on pages
Physical Science—Understand properties and changes of properties in matter.	36, 38
Physical Science—Understand transfer of energy.	39
Life Science—Understand structure and function in living systems.	21, 23, 25
Life Science—Understand diversity and adaptations of organisms.	28
Earth and Space Science—Understand structure of the earth system.	31, 33
Earth and Space Science—Understand Earth in the solar system.	35
Science in Personal and Social Perspectives—Understand populations, resources, and environments.	29

SOCIAL STUDIES	Standards are covered on pages
Understand the ways human beings view themselves in and over time.	41
Understand the interactions among people, places, and environments.	45
Understand individual development and identity.	40, 43
Understand how people create and change structures of power, authority, and governance.	47

Understand how people organize for the production, distribution, and consumption of goods and services.	49
Understand relationships among science, technology, and society.	52, 56, 58
Understand the ideals, principles, and practices of citizenship in a democratic republic.	46, 51

LANGUAGE ARTS	Standards are covered on pages
Apply a wide range of strategies to comprehend, interpret, evaluate, and appreciate texts. Draw on prior experience, interactions with other readers and writers, knowledge of word meaning and of other texts, word identification strategies, and understanding of textual features (e.g. sound-letter correspondence, sentence structure, context, graphics).	59, 68, 72
Employ a wide range of strategies while writing, and use different writing process elements appropriately to communicate with different audiences for a variety of purposes.	65, 75
Apply knowledge of language structure, language conventions (e.g. spelling and punctuation), media techniques, figurative language, and genre to create, critique, and discuss print and nonprint texts.	61, 63, 66, 70, 76, 79

Introduction

As a teacher who has adopted the differentiated philosophy, you design instruction to embrace the diversity of the unique students in your classroom and strategically select tools to build a classroom where all students can succeed. This requires careful planning and a very large toolkit! You must make decisions about what strategies and activities best meet the needs of the students in your classroom at that time. It is not a "one size fits all" approach.

When planning for differentiated instruction, include the steps described below. Refer to the planning model in *Differentiated Instructional Strategies: One Size Doesn't Fit All, Second Edition* (Gregory & Chapman, 2007) for more detailed information.

1. Establish standards, essential questions, and expectations for the lesson or unit.

2. Identify content, including facts, vocabulary, and essential skills.

3. Activate prior knowledge. Preassess students' levels of readiness for the learning and collect data on students' interests and attitudes about the topic.

4. Determine what students need to learn and how they will learn it. Plan various activities that complement the learning styles and readiness levels of all students in this particular class. Locate appropriate resources or materials for all levels of readiness.

5. Apply the strategies and adjust to meet students' varied needs.

6. Decide how you will assess students' knowledge. Consider providing choices for students to demonstrate what they know.

Differentiation does not mean always tiering every lesson for three levels of complexity or challenge. It *does* mean finding interesting, engaging, and appropriate ways to help students learn new concepts and skills. The practical activities in this book are designed to support your differentiated lesson plans. They are not prepackaged units but rather activities you can incorporate into your plan for meeting the unique needs of the students in your classroom right now. Use these activities as they fit into differentiated lessons or units you are planning. They might be used for total group lessons, to reinforce learning with individuals or small groups, to focus attention, to provide additional rehearsal opportunities, or to assess knowledge. Your differentiated toolkit should be brimming with engaging learning opportunities. Take out those tools and start building success for all your students!

Put It Into Practice

Differentiation is a Philosophy

For years teachers planned "the lesson" and taught it to all students, knowing that some will get it and some will not. Faced with NCLB and armed with brain research, we now know that this method of lesson planning will not reach the needs of all students. Every student learns differently. In order to leave no child behind, we must teach differently.

Differentiation is a philosophy that enables teachers to plan strategically in order to reach the needs of the diverse learners in the classroom and to help them meet the standards. Supporters of differentiation as a philosophy believe:

- All students have areas of strength.

- All students have areas that need to be strengthened.

- Each student's brain is as unique as a fingerprint.

- It is never too late to learn.

- When beginning a new topic, students bring their prior knowledge base and experience to the new learning.

- Emotions, feelings, and attitudes affect learning.

- All students can learn.

- Students learn in different ways at different times.

The Differentiated Classroom

A differentiated classroom is one in which the teacher responds to the unique needs of the students in that room, at that time. Differentiated instruction provides a variety of options to successfully reach targeted standards. It meets learners where they are and offers challenging, appropriate options for them to achieve success.

Differentiating Content By differentiating content the standards are met while the needs of the particular students being taught are considered. The teacher strategically selects the information to teach and the best resources with which to teach it using different genres, leveling materials, using a variety of instructional materials, and providing choice.

Differentiating Assessment Tools Most teachers already differentiate assessment during and after the learning. However, it is equally important to assess what knowledge or interests students bring to the learning formally or informally.

Assessing student knowledge prior to the learning experience helps the teacher find out:

- What standards, objectives, concepts, skills the students already understand

- What further instruction and opportunities for mastery are needed

- What areas of interests and feelings will influence the topic under study

- How to establish flexible groups—total, alone, partner, small group

Differentiating Performance Tasks In a differentiated classroom, the teacher provides various opportunities and choices for the students to show what they've learned. Students use their strengths to show what they know through a reflection activity, a portfolio, or an authentic task.

Differentiating Instructional Strategies When teachers vary instructional strategies and activities, more students learn content and meet standards. By targeting diverse intelligences and learning styles, teachers can develop learning activities that help students work in their areas of strength as well as areas that still need strengthening.

Some of these instructional strategies include:

- Graphic organizers

- Cubing

- Role-playing

- Centers

- Choice boards

- Adjustable assignments

- Projects

- Academic contracts

When planning, teachers in the differentiated classroom focus on the standards, but also adjust and redesign the learning activities, tailoring them to the needs of the unique learners in each classroom. Teachers also consider how the brain operates and strive to use research-based, best practices to maximize student learning. Through differentiation we give students the opportunity to learn to their full potential. A differentiated classroom engages students and facilitates learning so all learners can succeed!

CHAPTER 1

Mathematics

The Data Sisters

Standard
Data Analysis and Probability—Formulate questions that can be addressed with data, and collect, organize, and display relevant data to answer them.

Strategy
Metaphor

Objective
Students will learn metaphors to help them remember the terms *mean, median, mode,* and *range*.

Metaphors allow students to connect new information to more familiar concepts. To help students remember *mean, median, mode,* and *range*, introduce them to the Data Sisters. Act out the following scene with students, writing relevant terms on the board.

An: *Do you know **me**? **An**? I'm the oldest sister. My sisters sometimes say I'm bossy and **mean**, but really, I'm just **average**. To get to know me, you just add the numbers and divide that sum by the number of numbers. That's me, An!*

Dian: *Now it's time for **me, Dian**. I'm the middle child. No matter what, I'm always in the middle. I never even get to sit next to the car window. Whenever numbers are arranged in order, I'm the one in the middle. That's me, Dian.*

Mode: *I'm **Mode**, the youngest sister. I am a famous **mode**l. My picture is on magazine covers more often than any other number. Whatever number occurs most often, it's me, the famous model, Mode.*

An: *We sisters always argue about what car to drive. Personally, I like taking the Range Rover. It gets the best gas mileage from the least number to the greatest number. As you know, the **range** is the difference between the greatest number and the least number.*

Ideas for More Differentiation
Visual/spatial learners will enjoy drawing pictures to represent the Data Sisters.

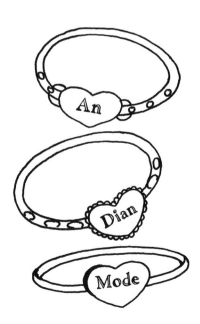

Please My Dear Aunt Sally

Strategies

Rehearsal

Mnemonics

Standard

Algebra—Understand patterns, relations, and functions.

Objective

Students will create a mnemonic device to remember the order of operations for solving algebraic equations.

A rehearsal activity is one in which students process in working memory. Mnemonics is a rehearsal strategy that associates easily remembered phrases with initial letters representing the information that needs to be retrieved. Verbal/linguistic learners in particular will enjoy using mnemonics.

For solving problems involving two or more operations, mathematicians have agreed that the operations should be performed in a certain order. (1) Do all operations inside parentheses. (2) Do all multiplication and division, moving from left to right. (3) Do all addition and subtraction, from left to right. So, the order is: **P**arentheses, **M**ultiplication, **D**ivision, **A**ddition, and **S**ubtraction.

To help students remember the order of operations, invite them to create a simple phrase (or mnemonic). For example, *Please My Dear Aunt Sally* is simple and makes sense syntactically. Tell students to avoid using words that don't make a phrase, such as *Pizza, Muffins, Donuts, Applesauce, Spaghetti*, because the order is too hard to remember.

Perhaps students can make a phrase that has special meaning in their lives, such as *Play Music Daily And Sing!* Or, they can use a classmate's name in their phrase, such as *Paul Might Dive And Swim*. Emphasize to students that creating a phrase that is meaningful to them will help them remember.

Ideas for More Differentiation

Invite students to work with a partner to create a phrase and then make a poster to illustrate it.

That's an Order!

Standard

Data Analysis and Probability—Select and use appropriate statistical methods to analyze data.

Objective

Students will play a game that provides practice with ordered pairs.

Materials

index cards
chalk

Making math fun is helpful to all types of learners. This game, played like the children's favorite "Red Light, Green Light," helps students visualize the way points move along the x-axis and y-axis on a graph. It will especially motivate kinesthetic learners, who like to move and learn at the same time.

1. Ahead of time, write many graph coordinates on index cards. To provide the greatest challenge, include ordered pairs with negative numbers, such as (–3, 2). For this coordinate, students will move left three steps and forward two steps.

2. To play the game, take students out to the playground. A basketball court works well, as the lines help form an imaginary graph. If you have a large class, divide the class into two groups and use two grids. Using chalk, draw one or two large coordinate grids on the blacktop.

3. Invite players to line up in a row along the bottom of the grid while the caller stands at the top. Give the caller a stack of coordinate index cards.

4. The caller begins by calling out a coordinate such as (5, 4). One player steps onto the grid, and other players help him or her find the right coordinate. The caller continues calling coordinates until the player is close enough to tag him or her. This player gets to be the next caller.

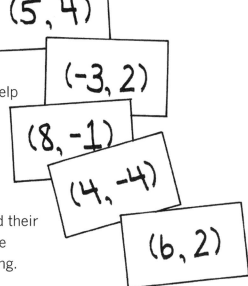

Ideas for More Differentiation

Divide students into even smaller groups, and allow them to find their own space on the playground to play the game. This allows more students to be callers and enjoy small-group, cooperative learning.

Graph It!

Standard
Problem Solving—Apply and adapt a variety of appropriate strategies to solve problems.

Objective
Students will work in cooperative groups to create a survey and develop graphs that depict the data.

Materials
12" x 18" white construction paper
crayons or markers

Students enjoy conducting surveys at home, in the classroom, and around school. The following activity integrates this interpersonal skill with mathematics.

1. Group students into cooperative learning groups of four, and assign each student one of the following jobs:
   - Materials Manager (manages supplies)
   - Recorder (writes survey)
   - Production Manager (makes sure that everyone knows what to do and that the product is accurate)
   - Time Manager (makes sure jobs are completed on time)

2. Instruct each group to write a survey and display the information gathered from the survey in graph form. The survey can relate to another curricular area (e.g., favorite book character, favorite inventor or scientist, favorite historical figure) or to their personal opinions or preferences (e.g., favorite movie, worst cafeteria food).

3. Have students write the survey question and decide if it will be multiple-choice or open-ended. Then they will decide on the number of people to survey. They can survey family members, classmates, or other students in the school. Instruct them to question their subjects and then tally the responses.

   For example, if students survey 30 classmates about the worst cafeteria food, they might ask: *What is the worst cafeteria food that should never be served again?* This survey question could be open-ended with no choices provided. The group tally sheet might look like this:

What is the worst cafeteria food that should never be served again?	
Nachos	IIII
Cold Grilled Cheese	II
Meatloaf Surprise	IIII I
Tuna Treat	IIII III
Cubed Beef on Toast	IIII

4. Students will then work together to create a graph that best depicts the information gathered. Provide several sample graphs from which students can choose (e.g., line graph, pictograph, bar graph, pie graph). Remind students to write the survey question on the graph.

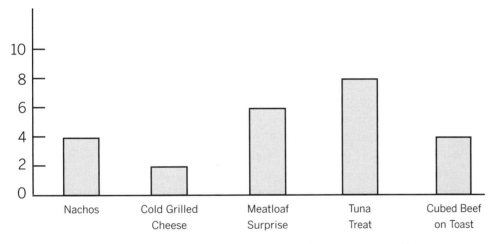

5. Finally, instruct each group to write a conclusion based on the information from the graph. For example: *Based on our survey results, Tuna Treat should be removed from the cafeteria menu.*

Ideas for More Differentiation

Challenge students to create more than one kind of graph to depict survey results.

Mental Math

Standard

Numbers and Operations—Compute fluently, and make reasonable estimates.

Objective

Students will mentally compute answers to equations.

A great focus activity for getting students ready for math is to engage them in some mental math. Begin even when students are cleaning up from a previous activity; it will get them centered and thinking before you know it.

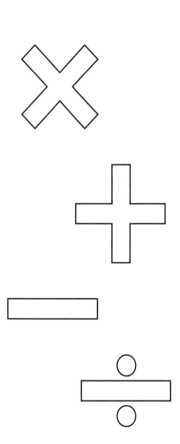

1. As students are cleaning up or getting ready for recess, say: *I'm going to start mental math!* (Have a small reward ready.)

2. Tell students that they may not raise their hands to answer until you say: *Equals!* Start by saying aloud a continuous problem, such as:

   7 times 4 (pause)

   Plus 3 (pause)

   Minus 6 (pause)

   Divided by 5 (pause)

   Times 8 (pause)

   Equals!

3. Choose the first student who raises his or her hand after you say *equals.* Take all answers until someone says the correct answer *(40).* Give that student a small reward.

4. Continue with another problem. You'll find that students scramble to get ready for the next mental challenge.

Ideas for More Differentiation

Adjust problems to suit students' abilities; give beginning mastery students fewer steps or easier problems. Give students with a high degree of mastery more steps or more difficult computations.

Puzzle It Out

Standard
Geometry—Analyze characteristics and properties of two- and three-dimensional shapes, and develop mathematical arguments about geometric relationships.

Objective
Students will design congruent-shapes worksheets and allow classmates to complete them.

Materials
boxes of different-sized puzzle pieces
drawing paper
pencils
crayons

This activity works great as two separate center activities on consecutive days. At the center, provide boxes of different-sized puzzle pieces, drawing paper, pencils, and crayons.

1. For the first day's center, invite students to choose several puzzle pieces and trace each of them two or three times on the paper. Direct students to turn each puzzle piece in a different direction or position each time they trace it. Tell them to trace as many shapes as will fit on the paper.

2. For the following day's center, put out all the papers students completed with traced puzzle pieces. Instruct students to take one of the papers, find the congruent shapes (same size, same shape), and then color the congruent shapes the same color.

Ideas for More Differentiation
Have beginning mastery students use only one puzzle piece to trace several times in different positions, and then fill the rest of the page with puzzle pieces that don't match. Have students with a high degree of mastery cut out the shapes after they color them and glue them onto black construction paper. They can place all congruent shapes in a row but not necessarily in the same position to create a tessellation.

Fraction Frenzy

Standard

Numbers and Operations—Understand numbers, ways of representing numbers, relationships among numbers, and number systems.

Objective

Students will play a game to practice identifying improper and equivalent fractions and fractions in their simplest form.

Materials

note cards
music recording
CD or cassette player

Teach to students' multiple intelligences by playing this engaging fraction identification game. Prior to the activity, write a set of fractions on note cards, including improper and equivalent fractions and fractions in their simplest form. Then make another set of three note cards reading *improper fractions, equivalent fractions,* and *simplest form.* Make enough cards so that each student gets one.

1. To play the game, give each student a fraction card, and play some music. While the music is playing, direct students to search for their group. For example, students with *improper fractions* look for each other as well as the person who has the card labeling their group (*improper fractions*). The object of the game is for everyone to find their group before the music ends.

2. When students find others in their group, direct them to hold on to each other's cards, making a fraction chain. There is one rule: The fractions in the *simplest form* group cannot be part of the *equivalent fractions* group (e.g., 1/3 must go with *simplest form*; it cannot join 2/6 in *equivalent fractions*).

Ideas for More Differentiation

Have beginning mastery students work in pairs with one card. They can work together to find their group. Give students with a high degree of mastery two cards each. Before they can link with other group members, they must trade cards with other students until they have two cards that belong in the same group. If there is no one left to trade cards with, they must trade cards with you (be sure to have lots of cards available).

McCentives

Standard
Numbers and Operations—Compute fluently, and make reasonable estimates.

Strategy
Structured project

Objective
Students will perform calculations to discover the percentage of daily calories in fast foods.

Materials
Fast Food Figures reproducible
calculators

Students today are inundated with marketing for fast food. With the ever-increasing pace of their families' lives, they are probably eating fast food more than they should. This activity will motivate students to think more carefully about what they order the next time they eat at a fast food restaurant.

1. To prepare for the activity, give students the following information:
   - Boys ages seven to ten require an average of 1,970 calories per day, while girls in the same age range require 1,740 calories.
   - Boys ages eleven to fourteen require an average of 2,220 calories per day, while girls in the same age range require 1,845 calories.

   These numbers may seem high to students at first, until they learn that 20 chicken nuggets from McDonald's contain 1,009 calories! For example, for a hungry ten-year-old boy, one meal of 20 chicken nuggets alone equals 51% of his required daily calories.

2. Next, invite students to explore the caloric content of their favorite fast foods on the Internet, using the key words *calories* andf *fast food*. This will direct them to Web sites that give specific information about foods from different fast food restaurants.

3. Tell students to calculate percentages of daily calories by dividing the total daily calories into the number of calories for a particular food and then multiplying that number by 100. For the chicken nuggets, divide 1,009 by 1,970, which equals .5121. Then multiply that number by 100 to get roughly 51%.

Fast Food Figures Page 19

4. To get students started, go to the board, and list the caloric content of some well-known fast foods. Invite them to use the **Fast Food Figures reproducible (page 19)** to organize the information. Encourage students to compute manually. Provide calculators for additional practice.

McDonald's
Bacon and Egg McMuffin (300 calories)
Big Mac (490 calories)

Burger King
Whopper (690 calories)
Cheeseburger (367 calories)

Pizza Hut
1 piece stuffed crust cheese pizza (271 calories)

Ideas for More Differentiation
Challenge students with a high degree of mastery to determine what fraction of the total daily calories a food contains.

Name _____   Date _____

Fast Food Figures

Directions: Use the chart to compare the calories in each food to the recommended daily calories.

Daily Calories Needed:		Boys	Girls
Ages 7 to 10		1,970	1,740
Ages 11 to 14		2,220	1,845
Food Item	**Restaurant**	**Calories**	**% of Daily Needs**

Using these foods, put together a typical meal you might eat. Add the calories of each item, and calculate the total percentage of calories in the meal compared to the recommended daily calories.

Food Item	Calories	% of Daily Needs

Total Calories in Meal: _____   Total % of Daily Needs: _____

Sounding Off with Rounding Off

Standard

Numbers and Operations—Understand numbers, ways of representing numbers, relationships among numbers, and number systems.

Objective

Students will use number cards to round whole numbers and decimals.

Materials

note cards
hole punch
key rings

This activity encourages students to experience place value and rounding in a completely new way.

1. To prepare for the activity, make five sets of note cards. On each set, write the numbers 0–9, one digit per card. Punch a hole in the bottom of each card, and attach each set with a key ring so students can flip through the cards. Make three additional cards: a decimal point, a comma, and an arrow.

2. To begin, say a number such as *5,842*. Call five students to the front of the room. Give four students a set of flip cards, and give one student the comma. Have students form the number by holding their cards and lining up in the correct order.

3. Choose a student to round off the number, and give him or her the arrow card. Tell the student, for example: *Round off to the nearest hundred*. The student points the arrow to his classmate in the hundreds place, and says: *Tia is in the hundred's place. She stands for 800*. Tia responds with: *Look to the number on the right. Is it less than 5, or 5 or greater?*

4. The student in the tens place says: *I am 4. I am less than 5*. This is when the whole class must either shout *round up* or *round down*. In this case, they would shout: *Round down!* The students holding the *4* and the *2* flip their cards to *0*. The new number will be 5,800.

5. Repeat this activity several times, starting with new numbers. Invite volunteers to take turns with the flip cards at the front of the class.

Ideas for More Differentiation

Divide the class into mixed-ability groups. Adjust the difficulty level of the numbers, for example, use smaller numbers or decimals.

CHAPTER 2

Science

Eggstraordinary Cells

Standard
Life Science—Understand structure and function in living systems.

Objective
Students will use metaphor to understand the parts of a cell.

Materials
overhead projector and transparency
raw eggs
small candies
jellybeans
clear plastic cup
chart paper

Strategies
Metaphor

Center activity

This activity uses metaphor to capture students' attention and keep them focused as they learn about cell structure. Using metaphor helps students connect new information to more familiar objects.

1. To begin the lesson, place a transparency on the overhead. Hold up the egg, and tell students: *This egg is like a cell. The eggshell is like the **cell membrane**—a thin covering that encloses the cell and holds the cell parts together. It also separates the cell from its surroundings.*

2. Carefully crack the raw egg onto the transparency. Point out the yolk, and continue: *The yolk is like the **nucleus** of the cell. It controls the cell's activities. It has its own membrane (point out the edge of the yolk). One function of the nucleus is cell reproduction. Inside the nucleus are **chromosomes**, which contain information about the characteristics of the organism.*

3. Point out the egg white: *Between the cell membrane and the nucleus is the **cytoplasm**, a jelly-like substance containing many chemicals to keep the cell functioning.*

4. Drop a few small candies into the egg white, and continue: *There are several kinds of **organelles** (structures within the cell that have their own particular function) in the cytoplasm, each with its*

own membrane. One of these organelles is called mitochondria. **Mitochondria** *release energy from food.*

5. Drop a few jellybeans into the egg white: *Other important organelles include the* **vacuoles**. *These are for storage; they store food, water, and waste materials.*

6. Next, distinguish between a plant cell and an animal cell: *A plant cell has a rigid cell wall as well as a membrane.* (Place an uncracked egg into a clear plastic cup to emphasize the point.) *A plant cell also contains an organelle called* **chloroplasts**, *which make food.* (Put more jellybeans into the egg white.)

7. At this point, invite students to draw what they see. Use chart paper to draw a model for students to follow, and label the parts. For more information about cell structure, go to the Cells Alive! Web site at: *http://www.cellsalive.com.* Here students can interact with animal and plant cell models.

8. When everyone is finished, throw away the egg. Then ask for a volunteer or two to come up to the overhead and retell your cell story using another egg and a clean transparency. Encourage and assist students with vocabulary and definitions as needed.

Ideas for More Differentiation

Invite students of mixed abilities to work in center groups. Give each group its own eggs and candies to create a cell model on a paper plate. They can then each experience observing, touching, and drawing it from a closer perspective.

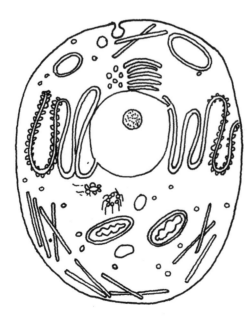

Animal Cell

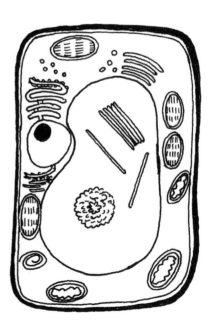

Plant Cell

Acting Out Passive Transport

Standard

Life Science—Understand structure and function in living systems.

Objective

Students will act out the concept of diffusion.

Materials

9 hula-hoops (or lengths of yarn tied in large circles)
note cards

Strategies
Rehearsal

Role play

Learning science from a textbook can become mundane. This activity invites students to act out ideas that they would normally learn straight from a textbook.

1. Before you begin the activity, explain the process of passive transport to students. Draw an accompanying diagram on the board, if needed:

   Passive transport is the energy-free movement of materials through a cell membrane. Diffusion is a process of passive transport. In diffusion, particles of a substance move from an area where there are many particles of the substance to an area where there are fewer particles of the substance. Diffusion takes place through the cell membrane, which acts as a filter, allowing some particles to pass through while keeping other particles out. Diffusion takes place when we breathe, inhaling oxygen and exhaling carbon dioxide.

2. Invite students to role-play the transfer of oxygen into cells and carbon dioxide out of cells during inhaling and exhaling. To begin, place eight hula-hoops or yarn circles on the floor (or out on the playground, where you will have more space). Spread out the hoops so they are about one foot apart. (You could also draw the circles with chalk.) These circles represent an animal's tissue cells.

3. Give half of the class note cards marked with an *O* for oxygen, and give the other half cards labeled CO_2 for carbon dioxide. Have the O students form a line behind one student who is holding up a hula-hoop. This hula-hoop represents the lungs. Meanwhile, the CO_2 students step into the hula-hoop tissue cells on the ground.

4. At your signal, the O students step through the "lungs" and move in a circle around the hula-hoop cells. Point out that this moving line represents the bloodstream.

5. As the O students circle the tissue, shout: *Diffuse!* At this point, O students move into the hula-hoop cells. They must make sure that each cell has oxygen! This demonstrates how oxygen diffuses out of red blood cells into other body cells.

6. While oxygen is moving into the cells, CO_2 students move out of the cells into the bloodstream. Tell the CO_2 students to move from the cells and step through the hula-hoop lungs, as they are being exhaled.

7. After all the CO_2 students have moved through the lungs, they make their way back into the cells, while the O students merge out into the bloodstream again. Instruct them to line up to go through the lungs and start the process all over again!

Ideas for More Differentiation

Appeal to students' musical intelligence by singing a jingle describing the process of diffusion. Sing the following lyrics to the tune of "The Hokey Pokey":

The oxygen comes in,
The CO_2 goes out,
The oxygen diffuses
To all the cells about.
Through the cell membranes
Particles can move.
That's what it's all about!

Digestive System Buddies

Standard
Life Science—Understand structure and function in living systems.

Objective
Students will create a life-sized diagram of the digestive system.

Materials
The Digestive System reproducible
diagram of the digestive system
butcher paper, construction paper
black markers, glue, scissors

Strategy
Energizing partners

After completing a lesson on the digestive system, inspire students' creativity by having them create two-dimensional models. If possible, pair artistic students with less artistic students to spread the wealth of artistic insight!

1. Provide students with a life-sized outline of a human torso. Make sure to include a profile of the head with the mouth open.

2. Have student pairs study a diagram of the digestive system. They will use construction paper to draw and cut out each part of the system (mouth, esophagus, liver, gallbladder, stomach, pancreas, large and small intestines, villi), and glue them onto the outline.

3. Direct students to label each part with marker and use **The Digestive System reproducible (page 27)** to describe its function. They can cut out each description and glue it under the label on their model. These digestive system parts should be included on the model:

   Mouth: Breaks food into smaller pieces to be swallowed; saliva secreted by glands helps moisten food and break down starches. Food then passes into the esophagus.

   Esophagus: A long tube that leads from the mouth to the stomach.

   Stomach: An organ that resembles a sack; it produces gastric juices, which contain acid and chemicals that break down protein. Food stays here for several hours before it passes into the small intestine.

   Small Intestine: Completes the digestion of food into nutrients by producing more chemicals; contains *villi* (projections sticking

The Digestive System Page 27

out of its walls), through which nutrients diffuse into the blood. Undigested food passes into the large intestine.

Large Intestine: Water and minerals are absorbed back into the bloodstream; waste passes through the large intestine and out of the body.

Liver: Produces bile, a chemical that breaks down fats into smaller particles that can be more easily digested.

Gallbladder: Stores bile produced by the liver.

Pancreas: Secretes juices into the small intestine and hormones into the bloodstream to aid in digestion.

Ideas for More Differentiation

Verbal/linguistic learners might enjoy role-playing to explain each part in the digestive process. (E.g., *I am the liver. My job is to produce bile.*) As each student speaks, he or she could tape the part to the appropriate section of the model.

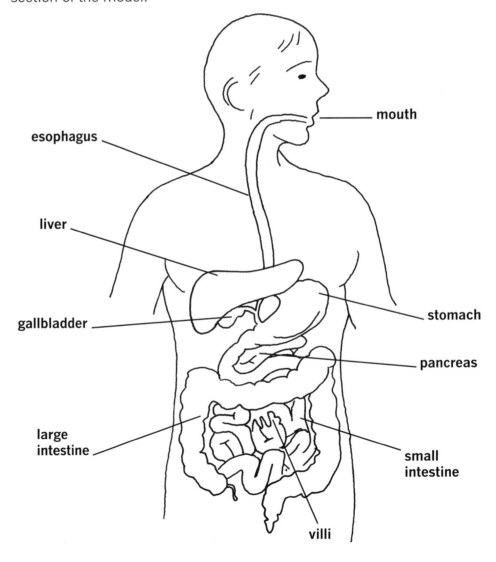

The Digestive System

Directions: Describe the function of each part of the digestive system. Then cut out the labels and glue them to your model.

Mouth	Esophagus	Stomach
Small Intestine	**Villi**	**Large Intestine**
Liver	**Gallbladder**	**Pancreas**

Vastly Vascular

Strategy
Multiple intelligences

Standard
Life Science—Understand diversity and adaptations of organisms.

Objective
Students will go on a "plant hunt" looking for, identifying, and recording their findings about vascular and nonvascular plants.

Materials
drawing paper
clipboards
potted vascular plants
magnifying glass

In fifth grade, students learn to distinguish between the two groups of plants: vascular and nonvascular. In their roots, stems, and leaves, *vascular plants* have tubes through which water and nutrients travel. *Nonvascular plants* do not have tubes. Water and nutrients must soak into the plants and pass from cell to cell. These plants, which include algae, moss, and fungi, must live in damp places. They do not have roots, stems, or true leaves.

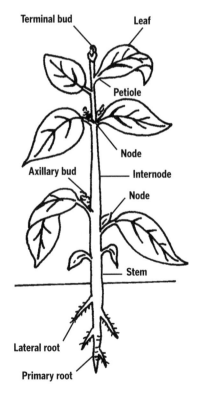

1. Invite students to go on a nature walk around campus to identify plants. Are the plants vascular or nonvascular? How do students know? Tell them to look for roots, stems, and leaves. If they find moss, they can pull up a small section.

2. As students find and identify each plant, tell them to sketch it and write where they found it on campus (sunny location or shady, wet location). They will probably find more vascular plants since there are more than half a million types on earth.

3. Create a plant study center in the classroom. Provide several potted vascular plants. Allow students to carefully remove the plants from their containers and observe their structure using a magnifying glass. Have them draw and label the plant parts.

Ideas for More Differentiation
Invite students with a high degree of mastery to use the Internet to conduct additional research on vascular and nonvascular plants. Ask them to present their findings to the class.

How We Use Plants

Standard

Science in Personal and Social Perspectives—Understand populations, resources, and environments.

Objectives

Students will work in cooperative groups to create an oral presentation on the uses of plants.

Materials

How We Use Plants reproducible

Tell students they will work together to research and create an oral report on how people use plants. Assign each group a specific topic, such as the use of plants as food or medicine.

1. Place students in cooperative groups of four. Ask each group member to take responsibility for one of the following roles:
   - Project Coordinator (keeps group on task)
   - Information Coordinator (coordinates research)
   - Materials Manager (gathers materials)
   - Oral Report Coach (gives positive feedback during rehearsal)

2. Tell students to begin by gathering information. Each student should research independently and then share his or her findings with the group. The Project Coordinator makes sure each student contributes to the introduction, body, and conclusion.

3. The group then works together to decide on visual aids. They should also consider gathering real materials that relate to their report (e.g., plants, popcorn, cotton fabric). Allow plenty of time for groups to rehearse before presenting their reports to the class.

4. Give students a copy of the **How We Use Plants reproducible (page 30)**. Tell them to complete the graphic organizer while they listen to other groups present their reports. The graphic organizer then becomes a great study tool for a test.

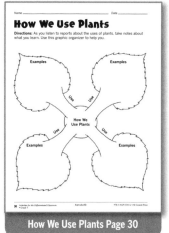

How We Use Plants Page 30

Name _____ Date _____

How We Use Plants

Directions: As you listen to reports about the uses of plants, take notes about what you learn. Use this graphic organizer to help you.

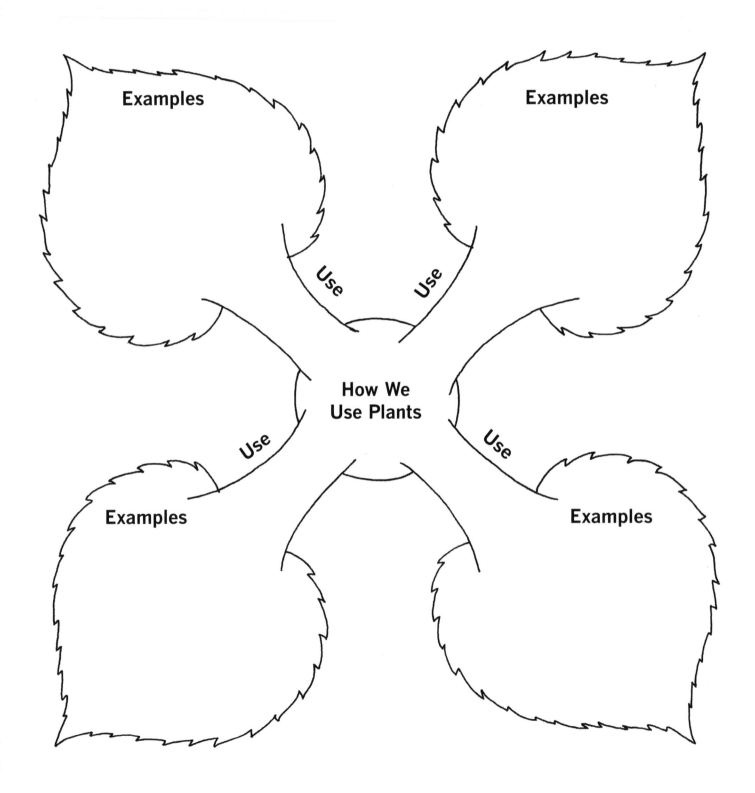

978-1-4129-5341-2 • © Corwin Press

A Scoop of Mesosphere

Standard
Earth and Space Science—Understand structure of the earth system.

Strategy
Metaphor

Objective
Students will build an ice cream sundae as a metaphor for Earth's atmosphere.

Materials
chocolate chip cookies
small candies
ice cream
hot fudge topping
bowls and spoons

Using metaphor allows students to connect what they are learning to something with which they are already familiar. Students will love this activity because they are quite familiar with ice cream!

1. Part of the fifth-grade science curriculum includes learning about Earth's atmosphere. Reinforce students' learning about the layers of Earth's atmosphere by introducing the following terms and connecting ideas.

   Scientists have divided the atmosphere into four distinct layers:

   Troposphere: The first layer, closest to Earth, is the *troposphere*. We live in this layer. We take *trop*ical vacations in the troposphere.

   Stratosphere: The second layer is the *stratosphere*. The stratosphere contains ozone, which protects Earth's creatures from the sun's harmful rays. People have used the *strat*egy of eliminating fluorocarbons from products such as hairspray to protect this ozone layer.

   Mesosphere: The third layer is the coldest, the *mesosphere*. People would be a *mess* if they had to live in the mesosphere.

   Thermosphere: The last layer is the *thermosphere*. It is the hottest layer, with a temperature reaching thousands of degrees Celsius. The classroom *thermo*meter would break if we had to measure the temperature of the thermosphere.

2. Help students remember each layer of Earth's atmosphere by having them create an atmospheric sundae. Invite students to a

table to create their own sundaes. They must ask for ingredients using the names of the atmospheric layers.

3. First, they put a chocolate chip cookie (*troposphere*) in the bowl. Then they sprinkle candies (*stratosphere*) on top. Next, they place a scoop of ice cream (cold *mesosphere*) on top. Finally, they pour hot fudge (hot *thermosphere*) all over it. Relating each ingredient to a layer of the atmosphere helps students remember not only the properties of each layer, but also in which order they appear.

4. If students do not care for hot fudge or candies or if they want more of an ingredient, they must call it by its atmospheric name. For example: *No thank you, I don't care for any more stratosphere today. Would anyone like more thermosphere? I've got some left!*

5. Have students draw and label each layer of their atmospheric sundae. Tell them to draw lines between the layers showing how the sundae is a metaphor for Earth's atmosphere.

Ideas for More Differentiation

Ask students to create a mnemonic device to help them remember the layers of Earth's atmosphere. For example: *Twinkling Stars Make Trails* or *Tiny Spiders Munch Toast*.

Flippin' for Science

Standard
Earth and Space Science—Understand structure of the earth system.

Objective
Students will process in working memory and equate making pancakes to the water cycle.

Materials
pancake mix
large bowl
mixing spoon
electric griddle
spatula
paper cups
thin paper plates
forks, napkins
construction-paper placemats

Elaborative rehearsal activities are great strategies for helping students analyze and remember information. Certain concepts, such as the water cycle, can be difficult to understand because students can't physically, materially experience them. A rehearsal strategy is a great way to approach this kind of concept, as students can observe all parts of the water cycle in action.

1. Demonstrate the water cycle for students by creating a simple center. Have an adult present to operate the hot griddle and guide student observations. Begin by preheating the griddle. Allow students to follow the directions on the pancake-mix box and mix the batter for the number of students in the center. Make sure they note that water is in the batter.

2. Pour some batter into each student's paper cup. Invite students one by one to pour their batter onto the griddle. As the pancakes cook, point out the rising steam. Explain that when the water in the batter meets the hot griddle, it turns to water vapor. This process is called *evaporation*.

3. If appropriate, allow students to flip their pancakes and let them finish cooking. Then have them place their pancakes on paper plates and put their plates on construction-paper placemats. Don't let anyone eat yet!

4. Ask a volunteer to review what they've seen so far. (*Water met with heat and evaporated, and the hot water vapor rose up.*) After about a minute, ask students what happens to water vapor when it cools. Invite them to pick up their plates and look at the bottom of the plate and the construction paper. They should find water spots.

5. Prompt students with questions such as: *Where did the water come from?* Guide them to see that water is a result of *condensation*; the hot pancake met the cool plate, paper, and table. As the water vapor cooled, it turned back into a liquid.

6. Explain that if enough water gathers, it will drip down in the form of *precipitation*. This occurs as the force of gravity returns water to the earth's surface. At this point, invite students to eat and enjoy their pancakes.

7. When they're finished eating, instruct students to write in their journals about how the water cycle is evident in making pancakes. They should illustrate their explanations and label the parts of the water cycle (e.g., *evaporation—the steam rising from the pancakes*).

Ideas for More Differentiation

Encourage students to create their own water cycle example based on everyday experiences (e.g., *taking a hot shower makes water vapor condense on a cold mirror*). Ask them to describe what they saw and explain connections to the water cycle. They can also draw and label an accompanying picture or demonstrate for the class.

Focus on the Moon

Standard
Earth and Space Science—Understand Earth in the solar system.

Strategy
Focus activity

Objective
Students will listen to songs and/or lyrics about the moon and write a poem about the moon.

Materials
songs about the moon
CD or cassette player

To get your students intrigued before a lesson on the moon and its phases, engage them in this simple focus activity—learning songs about the moon.

1. Ahead of time, look up moon songs on the Internet. You'll discover Web sites that offer lyrics and music to songs such as "Blue Moon," "Carolina Moon," "It's Only a Paper Moon," "Dancin' in the Moonlight," "Moon River," and "Blue Moon of Kentucky."

2. Read some of the lyrics to students, and if possible, play some of the songs. Discuss why there might be so many songs about the moon. (*It's mysterious; it's beautiful; it watches over us at night; it's dependable.*) Discuss the meaning of the phrase b*lue moon* and why it appears in so many songs. (A blue moon is a second full moon in a calendar month. It occurs rarely, only about every two and a half years, hence the expression *once in a blue moon*.)

3. Invite students to write their own song or poem about the moon. Get them started with simple acrostic poems.
   For example:

   Maybe the light will shine   **M**y mother made me come
   Only for you tonight.   **O**ver here and ask if
   Oceans of love are yours.   **O**ne day you'd go out with me, so
   Near to you I must be.   **N**ow I'm asking: Will you?

Ideas for More Differentiation
Allow students to research the names given to the moon by ancient civilizations or other cultures. Or, invite them to investigate other cultural beliefs about the moon.

Marshmallow Matters

Strategy
Center activity

Standard

Physical Science—Understand properties and changes of properties in matter.

Objective

Students will compare a physical change to a chemical reaction while roasting a marshmallow.

Materials

large marshmallows
candles in holders (e.g., cups)
lighter
forks
potholders
napkins

Fifth-grade science curriculum includes instruction on changes in matter. Creating an authentic task in which students can actually see these changes firsthand will help reinforce the learning experience.

1. Reinforce previous learning about the changing states of matter. A physical change occurs when a substance changes states. For example, solids become liquids, liquids becomes solids, liquids become gases, and gases become liquids. A chemical change occurs when a new substance is produced as two or more substances interact.

2. Invite a small number of students to work in a teacher-directed center and observe how a physical change and a chemical reaction occur while roasting a marshmallow.

3. Invite each student to stick a large marshmallow on a fork and hold the fork with a potholder. Light each candle, and ask students to cook the marshmallow over the flame. Tell them to think aloud about their observations. Prompt them with questions such as: *What do you see? What is happening to the marshmallow?*

4. After students have had time to react and respond, explain what is happening to the marshmallow:

- The marshmallow changes shape as it melts. This is a physical change, from a solid to a liquid.
- The marshmallow is also changing color, from white to brown and perhaps even to black. This color change is a big clue that a chemical reaction is taking place. The energy from the flame breaks the bonds that hold the marshmallow together. The sugar in the marshmallow then reacts with the oxygen in the air; this reaction produces carbon dioxide and water. The black substance on the marshmallow is carbon that hasn't yet been burned. A change of color or the production of light, heat, or gas is evidence that a chemical change has taken place.

5. While you discuss the science of roasting marshmallows, allow students to carefully eat their marshmallows. Then prompt them to write about their experience in their science journals.

Ideas for More Differentiation

Students with limited writing skills might draw a diagram of the marshmallow being roasted. They could label the melting marshmallow *physical change* and the blackened part *chemical change*.

It's "Element"ary

Standard
Physical Science—Understand properties and changes of properties in matter.

Objective
Students will create cheers and odes to describe elements.

Materials
periodic table of elements

This motivating activity hooks students into learning the periodic table of elements by creating cheers and odes to reinforce basic information about each element.

Display a copy of the periodic table of elements. Then have each student choose an element to research using an encyclopedia or the Internet. They can find great information on the Radiochemistry Society Web site at: *www.radiochemistry.org.* Invite students to write a creative cheer or ode about or to their element using the information they researched. For example:

Cheer for Strontium
Strontium, you're great!
You're atomic number 38,
You're yellow and pale;
You're not natural.
You're found only in combination,
But you're a blast at a 4th of July celebration!

Ode to Aluminum
Aluminum, aluminum,
Unlucky number 13,
You combine so well with oxygen
That you are never pure in nature.
You're very common in Earth's crust,
Yet your silver sheen delights me.

Ideas for More Differentiation
Interpersonal learners may enjoy working with a partner to write and then their poem to the class. Other students can illustrate their poems and display them next to the periodic table of elements.

Follow the Foil

Standard
Physical Science—Understand transfer of energy.

Strategy
Role play

Objective
Students will create a human model of an electrical circuit.

Materials
rope or yarn
chairs

To help students better understand the flow of electricity through a circuit, invite them to act it out. This kind of role play especially engages kinesthetic learners as they move around the classroom.

1. To begin, unroll rope or yarn on the floor to make two different circuits. Place a positive sign (+) and a negative sign (–) at the beginning and end of each circuit. Make only one path for a series circuit, but make two paths for a parallel circuit. See the diagrams on the right.

2. Explain to students that the rope acts as the *conductor* (material that carries electrons easily). The rope is unrolled on the floor, so the floor is acting as the *insulator* (material that doesn't carry electrons). Normally, a wire would be the conductor, and the plastic coating around the wire would be the insulator.

3. Place some chairs along the rope path. Explain that these chairs will act as *resistors* (materials that resist electric current but don't stop it; they allow electric energy to be changed into other forms).

4. Students will be the *electrons*. They will follow the rope path as electricity flowing through the circuit. When they arrive at a resistor, they crawl underneath it or step over it. This shows how electricity follows a path between two terminals with opposite charges. The resistors don't stop the flow, but they do slow it down.

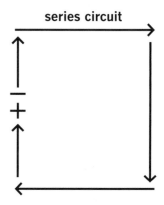

series circuit

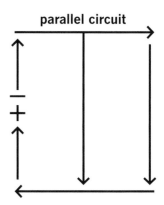

parallel circuit

Ideas for More Differentiation
To help beginning mastery students, talk them through the path, explaining each element along the way. Students with a high degree of mastery may explain what they are doing as they travel the circuit.

CHAPTER 3

Social Studies

Personal Artifacts

Strategy
Community cluster

Standard
Understand individual development and identity.

Objective
Students will collect three artifacts that represent themselves and prepare an oral presentation that describes the meaning of these artifacts.

In this activity, students will learn what artifacts can tell about an individual or culture, and they will also learn a lot about each other.

1. Explain to students that artifacts are objects made by humans. Archaeologists look for artifacts from ancient civilizations because they learn about the culture and way of life of the people who created them. Ask each student to bring in three items from home that tell something about their life or culture.

2. After everyone has brought in their artifacts, place students in groups of three. Have students display their artifacts on a table. Invite group members to study each other's artifacts and write their thoughts about what the artifacts represent on a sticky note. Have them place the notes on the table next to each item.

3. Have students return to their own artifacts and gather the accompanying sticky notes. Direct them to use these notes in an oral presentation about their artifacts. For example, a student may bring in a baseball, and a sticky note may read: *Jason must be in Little League.* When Jason gives his presentation, he might say: *You may think this baseball means I play sports, but it doesn't. This is the ball I caught at a Yankees game I went to with my dad.*

Ideas for More Differentiation
Students can prepare a written report rather than an oral presentation. Or, entice artistic students to draw their objects and write around the shapes to explain what they represent.

Daily Diary

Standard
Understand the ways human beings view themselves in and over time.

Objective
Students will keep a daily diary to record insights and primary source information.

Explain to students the difference between primary and secondary source information. Primary sources include written accounts, photographs, or even paintings created by people who saw or took part in an event. Secondary sources are records of events from someone who was not there at the time. The reason we have such detailed information about historical events is mostly due to primary sources.

1. Starting on the first day of school, invite students to keep a daily diary of what they experience at school. Encourage them to record opinions, feelings, and meaningful events in whcih they participate or that they witness firsthand. Tell students to date each entry. Caution students not to write anything in their diary that they would not want to share. These are personal, but not private, diaries.

2. After students have written for several weeks, ask them to go back in time. Choose a date from the past, and invite students to read their diary entry from that day. Invite students to share entries with partners or in small groups. Prompt them to discuss how their opinions and observations compare. Did they record similar events? Were their accounts of an event similar or different?

3. After discussion, bring the class together again. Relate the diaries to primary source information. Stress that although people may experience the same event, their versions of what happen may be completely different!

Ideas for More Differentiation
Students who have difficulty writing may record an event as a comic strip. Some students may want to choose a date from their notebooks and prepare an oral presentation about what historical events happened on the same date over many years or even centuries.

What Is a Hero?

Strategies

Cooperative group learning

Think-Pair-Share

Standard
Understand the interactions among people, places, and environments.

Objective
Students will evaluate whether Christopher Columbus was or was not a hero.

Materials
chart paper
markers

This is a great activity to launch students on a study of various world explorers. Begin your study with a class discussion about Christopher Columbus.

1. To begin, offer the following question to students for discussion: *What is a hero?* Have students Think-Pair-Share their responses.

2. Divide the class into groups of four, and choose one student to be the recorder. Give each group a piece of chart paper and a marker. Their mission is to define the word *hero* and give examples of heroes who illustrate their definitions. Have them post their papers around the room and read and compare the definitions.

3. Then ask students to determine if Christopher Columbus was a hero. Use Think-Pair-Share again. Have groups use the definitions from their charts to see if Columbus fits their descriptions.

4. Continue the discussion, and introduce point of view. Ask students: *Would the Spaniards in the late 1400s think Columbus was a hero? What about the Taino Indians of the same period?*

5. Finally, ask students to reflect on the discussion in their journals. Have them answer the question again: *Was Christopher Columbus a hero? Why or why not?*

Ideas for More Differentiation
Students who need more challenge may have a debate. Invite some students to present arguments for why Columbus was a hero, while others present arguments for why he was not.

History's Mysteries

Standard
Understand individual development and identity.

Objective
Students will role-play historical figures and play a game to guess who is portraying the real figure.

Materials
self-stick nametags

Strategies
Game

Role play

Do your students have a flair for the dramatic? If they do, they will enjoy this engaging, interactive game. Have students work in groups of three. Their task is to choose and research a famous figure from history (someone the class has already studied). One group member will accurately portray the figure while the other two students inaccurately portray the figure. This game is played similar to the television series "What's My Line?"

1. To play the game, have groups sit at the front of the class one at a time. Each student wears a nametag labeled *#1, #2,* or *#3*. Introduce the group as the historical figure (e.g., *I'd like to introduce you to the famous Ferdinand Magellan*).

2. Direct the rest of the class to ask questions of each group member to determine who is the real Magellan (#3). This really gives students a chance to ham it up! For example:

   Student: *Magellan #2, who paid for your expedition?*

   Magellan #2: The king of France. (This provides a clue that Magellan #2 is not the real Magellan, because the king of Spain supplied the funds.)

   Student: *Magellan #1, what was your purpose in traveling to South America?*

   Magellan #1: I wanted to find a route to Africa by sailing around the Americas. (This provides a clue that Magellan #1 is not the real Magellan, because he was actually looking for a route to Asia by way of the Americas.)

   Student: *Magellan #3, did you find a river that connected the Atlantic Ocean to the Pacific Ocean?*

Magellan #3: After many attempts at sailing up rivers that only ended in the middle of the continent, we finally found a path through the tip of South America. They even named this strait after me. (This provides a clue that this might be the real Magellan, since this answer is correct.)

3. Direct students to continue questioning the three Magellans until someone can conclusively identify the real Magellan. This student makes a guess and must provide reasons to support it.

4. Finally, tell all three Magellans: *Will the real Magellan please stand up!* The real Magellan dramatically stands up. If a student guesses correctly, he or she and the real figure are the winners. If a student guesses an imposter, the impostor is the winner!

Ideas for More Differentiation

Students may use notes to help them remember facts about the historical figure. The questioners may also want to work in pairs to brainstorm a list of questions for each figure.

Weighty Words

Standard
Understand the interactions among people, places, and environments.

Strategy
Focus activity

Objective
Students will discuss the meanings of quotations attributed to famous Americans.

Social studies textbooks are full of quotations from historical figures. However, those quotations are often glanced at and then bypassed. Exploring the meaning of a quotation can enrich a student's understanding of the time period and give insight into the person's personality, intentions, and goals.

1. As a focus activity, introduce a quotation. You can find a multitude of quotations on the Internet using the key words *famous American historical quotations.* (Find great quotations by famous historical figures as well as cultural figures such as writers, poets, actors, and singers.) Read the quotation aloud to students. Discuss the meaning of the quotation, and ask students to guess who said it.

2. Discuss the time period in which the quotation was made and the events occurring in America during that time. Prompt students with questions: *Does the quotation stand true today? What does the quotation say about the person who said it? What does it say about the values of American society at the time?* Consider allowing time for students to respond in their journals.

The following are some examples of famous quotations that are sure to provoke lively discussion in your classroom.

Abraham Lincoln: You cannot fail if you resolutely determine that you will not.

Thomas Jefferson: When the press is free, and every man able to read, all is safe.

Sojourner Truth: Truth burns up error.

Thomas Paine: If there must be trouble let it be in my day, that my child may have peace.

George Washington: Labor to keep alive in your breast that little spark of celestial fire called conscience.

We the People

Strategy
Cooperative group learning

Standard
Understand the ideals, principles, and practices of citizenship in a democratic republic.

Objective
Students will rewrite parts of the U.S. Constitution in their own words.

Materials
copies of the *United States Constitution*
note cards
chart paper
glue

Challenge students to analyze the Constitution in a new and different way with this cooperative-group activity.

1. Preassess students' readiness levels, and then create mixed-ability groups. Assign each group a passage of the Constitution to read and rewrite in their own words.

2. Instruct students to use note cards to restate each section in their own words. On chart paper, outline the document as you go along (*Preamble, Article I, Section 1, Section 2 (1), (2), (3)*, and so on). Students then glue the note cards on the appropriate section of the chart paper.

   For example, Section 3 (4) states: *The Vice President of the United States shall be President of the Senate, but shall have no vote, unless they be equally divided.* Students might rewrite this as: *The U.S. Vice President is also the President of the Senate. He doesn't get to vote, though, unless there is a tie in the Senate.*

3. You might consider starting this activity at the beginning of the year and making it an ongoing assignment. Students will rewrite the entire document in order (while you are still differentiating sections according to student readiness levels).

Ideas for More Differentiation
Students might benefit from using Internet resources to find meaning. Other students might enjoy adding visual representations of their ideas. Encourage all students to use their strengths for this assignment.

An Amazing American

Standard
Understand how people create and change structures of power, authority, and governance.

Objective
Students will conduct research about famous American women and design a way to share the information about her with their classmates.

Materials
Amazing American Woman reproducible

Sojourner Truth, Harriet Tubman, Abigail Adams, Dolly Madison, Pocahontas, Sacagawea, Elizabeth Cady Stanton, Rosa Parks, Sandra Day O'Connor, Sally Ride, and Maya Angelou are just a few of the many famous women in American history. In this activity, students feature these women in special, personalized presentations.

1. Challenge students to help you make a list of women who changed the world. They can search through their social studies texts, encyclopedias, or the Internet. They could also choose to conduct interviews or use another method.

2. Once a comprehensive list has been compiled, invite students to work individually or in pairs to choose and investigate the history of a woman from the list.

3. Provide a choice board from which students can choose a way to present their information. Display a wheel with a choice written in each section, for example: *oral report, short play or reenactment, storyboard or comic strip, poem or song, collage of important events, storytelling, symbolic representation.*

4. Give students a copy of the **Amazing American Woman reproducible (page 48)** to help them organize their information and plan their presentations.

Ideas for More Differentiation
Some students may enjoy working in cooperative groups of four. Make sure students are each assigned a task and actively participate.

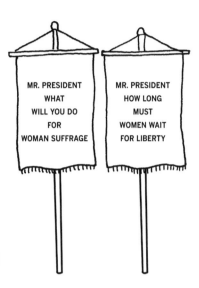

Amazing American Woman Page 48

Amazing American Woman

Directions: Use this graphic organizer to help you organize information for your presentation.

Woman's Name	Period in History	Year of Birth/Death

What problems did she face?

What did she do to solve these problems?

If you could ask her three questions, what would they be?

What makes her an important figure in American history?

Ad-miration

Standard
Understand how people organize for the production, distribution, and consumption of goods and services.

Strategy
Cooperative group learning

Objective
Students will examine an advertisement and trace the product's roots from consumer-readiness to its origin.

Materials
magazine ads
posterboard
art supplies

Before beginning the activity, invite students to bring in appropriate magazine advertisements they find interesting, funny, or especially effective. As a class, sort the ads into categories, such as *toothpaste, food, soft drinks,* and *clothing.*

1. Divide the class into cooperative groups of four. Give each group a category of ads to study. Tell group members to look at, analyze, and compare and contrast the ads.

2. Prompt students with questions such as: *What do you notice? Are the toothpaste ads covered with images of people with beautiful smiles and white teeth? What about the soda ads? Are they filled with pictures of young adults energetically participating in sports activities, such as rock climbing?*

3. Have students write down the attributes of each ad. Then have them write how the ads make them feel (e.g. *happy, envious, excited*). Ask students: *Does the ad make you want to purchase the product?*

4. When students are finished recording their observations, have them choose their favorite ad and use the Internet to research it. They should look for answers to some of the following questions: *What company made the product? Where is the company located? How long has it been doing business? How did the company begin? What ingredients are in the product? Are the ingredients local to the company's area?* For example, General Mills, the cereal manufacturer, is located in Minnesota, where rice, wheat, and corn are grown. It started as a flour mill in the late 1800s.

5. After students gather information about the product, direct them to use posterboard and art supplies to create another ad for it. But this time, the ads will be more realistic. For example, for a soda ad they can write: *It's lots of processed sugar and sweet corn syrup mixed with bubbly water in a pretty can!* They can draw what people would look like if they really indulged in drinking the product. (They would probably have rotten teeth and be too unhealthy to scale a mountain.)

6. Invite students to display their "reality ads" next to the magazine ads. Initiate a class discussion about how students feel about the products and the magazine ads after they've studied the products more thoroughly.

Ideas for More Differentiation
Students can advertise their products for the class in a report, a TV commercial, or an original jingle.

Symbolize America

Standard
Understand the ideals, principles, and practices of citizenship in a democratic republic.

Objective
Students will study and evaluate American symbols.

Materials
construction paper
crayons or markers

One important aspect of understanding American history is knowing about its symbols and how these symbols came to represent America.

1. Invite students to brainstorm a list of symbols they associate with America, such as the flag, the bald eagle, the Statue of Liberty, the Liberty Bell, Lincoln Memorial, Uncle Sam, the Capitol building, or Mount Rushmore.

2. Explore these symbols in depth by asking student pairs to research how they were chosen, created, or adopted into American culture. Encourage students to include interesting trivia, such as the fact that America's bald eagle is not really bald, but piebald, meaning two-colored. They should also include how the symbols represent American ideals (e.g., the eagle represents the freedom we hold so dear).

3. Invite pairs to choose an original way to share what they've learned, such as an oral presentation, poster or diagram, written report, poem, brochure, or short skit.

4. After students' presentations, discuss unconventional American symbols. Ask: *When you see a red and white Coca-Cola can or McDonald's golden arches, do you think "America"? Why or why not?* Encourage students to become active observers and energetic thinkers about American symbols and what each of those symbols really means.

Ideas for More Differentiation
Allow students to create their own American symbol and explain why they think their symbol embodies American culture and values.

My Life/Your Life

Strategies

Graphic organizer

Authentic task

Standard

Understand relationships among science, technology, and society.

Objective

Students will interview a parent, grandparent, or other adult to compare life today with life in the past.

Materials

My Life/Your Life reproducible
Compare and Contrast reproducible

My Life/Your Life Page 54

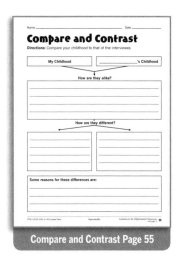

Compare and Contrast Page 55

Life in America has changed dramatically over the past century. An important aspect of the social studies curriculum is teaching students about how changes occur over time (particularly in technology) and how the past compares to the present. A simple but effective strategy for reinforcing this concept is having students compare their childhood today to an adult's childhood in the past.

The goal of this activity is to get students thinking about how technological advances change the way people live and communicate.

1. Give students a copy of the **My Life/Your Life reproducible (page 54)**. Invite students to complete the section titled *My Childhood*. They will answer questions about themselves.

2. Students will interview a parent, grandparent, or other adult one or two generations older (e.g., friend, neighbor, or relative). They will complete the section titled _____'s *Childhood*. (If students can't find a friend or relative to interview, find some school staff members who might want to participate, such as the librarian, secretary, nurse, or janitor.)

3. Ask students to bring in their completed interview sheets. Instruct them to compare the information in both columns and highlight answers that show similar experiences. Students will also find many things that are different.

4. Give students a copy of the **Compare and Contrast reproducible (page 55)**. Tell them to use this sheet to record the similarities and differences between their life and the interviewee's life.

5. Initiate a class discussion about these similarities and differences. Encourage students to think about the reasons their lives might be so different. Ask students: *Are the differences due to changes in*

technology? Are they due to the fact that you grew up in different countries? What accounts for the major differences in your lives, being that the time between your childhoods is not so vast?

6. Consider simple things such as the evolution from letters to e-mails for personal correspondence. Ask:*How does that affect the way people communicate and stay in touch with each other?* Discuss how the art of letter writing has been lost. E-mails are usually impulsive thoughts, while letters are crafted and pondered before they're sent.

7. To bring the experience to life, invite one or two willing parents or grandparents to visit your classroom and talk about their childhoods. Invite them to discuss the city or town where they grew up, how much they paid for food, what kind of transportation they used, what their school was like, and what toys and games they enjoyed.

My Life/Your Life

Directions: Answer questions about your life in the middle column. Record your interviewee's answers in the right column.

Questions	My Childhood	_____'s Childhood
1. Where did you grow up?		
2. How do/did you get to school?		
3. What tools do/did you use to do school work?		
4. What games and activities do/did you like?		
5. How do/did you communicate with family and friends?		
6. What kinds of meals do/did you enjoy?		
7. What do/did you do with your spare time?		
8. How many televisions are/were in your home?		
9. How many computers are/were in your home?		

Name _____ Date _____

Compare and Contrast

Directions: Compare your childhood to that of the interviewee.

My Childhood	_____'s Childhood

How are they alike?

_____

_____

_____

_____

How are they different?

_____ _____

_____ _____

_____ _____

Some reasons for these differences are:

_____

_____

_____

Intentions of Inventions

Strategy

Graphic organizer

Standard

Understand relationships among science, technology, and society.

Objective

Students will study the causes that led to and effects that resulted from particular inventions. They will make a diagram to show the cause-and-effect relationship.

Materials

Triangle Graphic Organizers reproducible
overhead projector and transparency

Cause-and-effect relationships are especially important in the study of history. Focus your lesson on the causes and effects of historical inventions. Explain to students that one thing always causes another. For every action (cause), there is a reaction (effect).

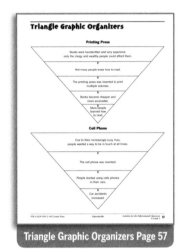

Triangle Graphic Organizers Page 57

1. Display a transparency of the **Triangle Graphic Organizers reproducible (page 57)**. Explain the connecting information and events to highlight the cause-and-effect relationships. Explain to students that they will be using a triangle graphic organizer to visually show how one event leads to another.

2. Invite student to work individually or in pairs to research one historically significant invention. They can choose an invention from the past (e.g., airplane, electricity, telescope) or one that is more recent (e.g., computer, video games, television).

3. Prompt students to create their own triangle graphic organizers to show the cause-and-effect relationships brought on by a chosen invention. Invite them to illustrate their organizers and display them on a bulletin board.

Triangle Graphic Organizers

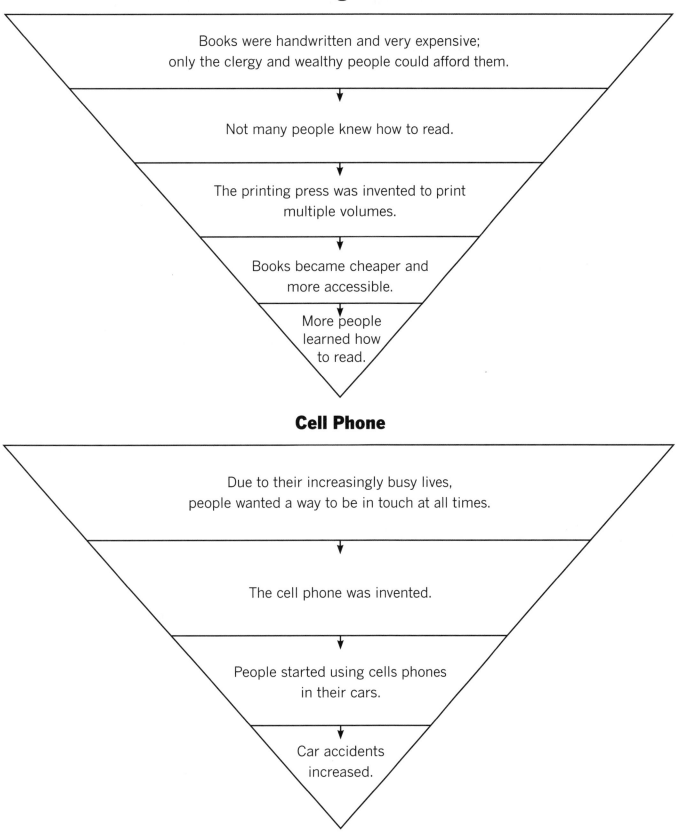

Printing Press

Books were handwritten and very expensive;
only the clergy and wealthy people could afford them.

Not many people knew how to read.

The printing press was invented to print
multiple volumes.

Books became cheaper and
more accessible.

More people
learned how
to read.

Cell Phone

Due to their increasingly busy lives,
people wanted a way to be in touch at all times.

The cell phone was invented.

People started using cells phones
in their cars.

Car accidents
increased.

Necessity's Child

Strategy
Open-ended project

Standard
Understand relationships among science, technology, and society.

Objective
Students will invent something that society needs and then describe their invention.

Materials
drawing paper
art supplies

Initiate a discussion based on the saying, *Necessity is the mother of invention*. Remind students of inventions that have helped people accomplish tasks more quickly or easily, such as electricity, computers, the printing press, the cotton gin, cars, and planes. Ask students to imagine other inventions that could improve our world. Encourage students to think like inventors!

1. Challenge students to brainstorm situations that people often complain about or are frustrated by. Ask: *Does it bother you when you see people throw trash out of their cars? Do you feel frustrated when you can't find the TV remote? Have you ever noticed a streetlight turn red before people with wheelchairs finish crossing the street? What can you do about these situations?*

2. Have students create a list of ways these situations and others could be improved. Invite them to brainstorm as a group and interview others to get more ideas. Direct them to choose one problem they want to fix and think about what they could invent to solve it.

3. Tell students to imagine that they have unlimited resources at their disposal to create their invention. Direct them to illustrate, name, and describe their inventions.

4. Invite students to present their inventions to the class. Have the class vote on which inventions are the most creative, most innovative, most needed, most likely to work, and so on.

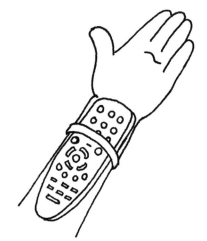

Remote Control Watch

Ideas for More Differentiation
Invite kinesthetic learners to build a prototype of their invention. Students who have difficulty writing may choose to present their inventions verbally.

CHAPTER 4

Language Arts

The View from Here

Standard

Apply a wide range of strategies to comprehend, interpret, evaluate, and appreciate texts. Draw on prior experience, interactions with other readers and writers, knowledge of word meaning and of other texts, word identification strategies, and understanding of textual features (e.g., sound-letter correspondence, sentence structure, context, graphics).

Strategy
Focus activity

Objective

Students will explore point of view in literature.

Materials

The True Story of the Three Little Pigs by Jon Scieska

Get students' attention by reading aloud the delightful book *The True Story of the Three Little Pigs* by Jon Scieszka, a picture book that tells the well-known story of *The Three Little Pigs* from the wolf's point of view. Then engage students in the following point-of-view focus activity to spark debate about story characters who never get a chance to speak for themselves.

1. To help students understand point of view, invite a volunteer to the front of the class where you sit or stand. Direct the student to look around the classroom to see what you see. Invite the student to discuss things he or she never noticed before.

2. Then switch places, and sit in the student's chair, observing the room from his or her perspective. What do you notice that you've never noticed before? Share your thoughts aloud with students.

3. Initiate a discussion about the story *Cinderella*. Ask students: *What if Prince Charming didn't want to get married? What if he wanted to be captain of a ship and sail to India? How would the story be different if Prince Charming were the narrator or if the reader experienced the story through his eyes?*

4. Explain that *point of view* refers to the identity of narrative voice, or the character through which the reader experiences the story. Point of view may be third person (omniscient narrator) or first person (narrated by a character in the story).

> For example, in *Cinderella,* the reader experiences Cinderella's view of the world. We learn that she is sad and overworked; she struggles to belong; she falls in love; and finally, she lives happily ever after. But we don't hear about Prince Charming's thoughts. What might he be thinking and experiencing?

5. Explain that to really get inside a story, students should try to examine the story's events from different characters' points of view. Here are some characters to consider:
   - Toto's or the Wicked Witch's point of view *(The Wizard of Oz)*
   - Dudley's point of view (Harry Potter books)
   - The pants' point of view *(The Sisterhood of the Traveling Pants)*
   - An Oompah Loompah's point of view *(Charlie and the Chocolate Factory)*

Ideas for More Differentiation

Challenge students to choose a well-known story to rewrite or act out in a short skit. Invite them to write from a different character's point of view.

Mighty Metaphors

Standard
Apply knowledge of language structure, language conventions, media techniques, figurative language, and genre to create, critique, and discuss print and nonprint texts.

Objective
Students will use metaphor to increase their understanding.

Materials
2 boxes
index cards

Metaphor is a common and very important element in understanding literature and increasing comprehension and vocabulary. Use this activity to help students practice using metaphors.

1. Before beginning the activity, invite each student to write several nouns on individual index cards. Tell them to include at least one person, one place, and one thing. Divide the cards equally into two different boxes.

2. Demonstrate the activity several times to make sure students understand how to do it. Draw a card from each box. You will have two nouns, for example, *teacher* and *road*. Write on the board: *teacher = road.*

3. Tell students that to create a metaphor, they use the word *is*. Compare *is* to the equals sign (=) in a math equation. Explain that according to I. A. Richards in *The Philosophy of Rhetoric* (1936), a metaphor consists of two parts—the *tenor* and the *vehicle*. The tenor is the subject to which attributes are given. The vehicle is the subject from which the attributes are borrowed.

4. Use a tenor and a vehicle with your first two nouns to create a metaphor, such as: *A teacher is a road to the world of knowledge. Travel along this road; follow where it takes you; and you will learn.*

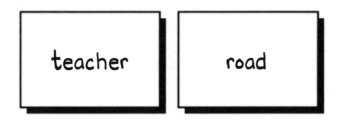

5. Draw two more nouns from the boxes, for example, *fear* and *rabbit*. Write on the chalkboard *fear = rabbit*. Then provide another example metaphor, such as: *His fear is a rabbit, dashing from one bush to another, eyes wide open, waiting for the grasp of talons from above.*

6. Provide another example metaphor, such as: *eyebrows = telephone poles: Eyebrows are telephone poles, punctuating the face of the street with brown, stark lines, conveying silent messages.*

7. After providing several examples, invite students to create their own metaphors. Ask students to choose nouns one at a time from the boxes. Depending on students' abilities and comfort levels, you may have them work individually or in pairs, or you can have them present metaphors verbally at the front of the class.

Ideas for More Differentiation

As students read, encourage them to keep a list of metaphors they find in text. Visual students may enjoy illustrating the components of metaphors (e.g., drawing eyebrows on a street or telephone poles on a face).

Searching for Symbols

Standard
Apply knowledge of language structure, language conventions, media techniques, figurative language, and genre to create, critique, and discuss print and nonprint texts.

Objective
Students will explore symbolism by creating symbols to represent their ideas.

Materials
magazines
scissors
art supplies
journals

Symbolism is the use of specific objects or images to represent abstract ideas. A symbol must be something visible or tangible. The idea it symbolizes must be something abstract or universal.

1. Initiate a class discussion about symbols. Point out that students see symbols every day, such as the American flag (symbolizing freedom) or the Nike swoosh (symbolizing speed and endurance).

2. Explain that symbolism is used frequently in movies and literature, especially poetry. For example, imagine the last scene of a movie about an overworked man's desperate attempt to escape his stressful life in New York City. The film ends with a wide-angle shot of a palm tree in the sand. Ask students: *What does that tree represent? A new beginning? An escape for a trapped man? A future filled with days at the beach?*

3. Give students some examples to get their creative juices flowing: a cup of hot coffee could represent hearth and home; a soaring bird could represent freedom. A rose could represent love or blood (red), purity of heart (white), or friendship (yellow).

4. Invite students to search for and find their own symbols. Provide magazines in which they can find pictures that would make good symbols. Have them cut out several pictures and glue them into a composition book to create a symbols journal. Have students

write what the symbols represent. Students may write from what they've experienced in their reading, or they can create their own meaning. Encourage students to create original symbols by drawing or using art supplies.

5. When students are finished, have them share their symbols with the class. Ask them: *Did anyone use the same symbol? Did it represent something different or something similar? Did everyone in the class make the same or different connections to the symbols presented?*

6. Use this activity as a starting point from which students can explore symbols around them. Invite students to look for symbols in books they read or movies they see and take note in their symbols journal. They can continue to collect and record symbols they find meaningful and relevant to their lives.

Ideas for More Differentiation

Students can work in pairs to determine symbols' meanings. They could also interview classmates or family members to determine how symbols change in their meaning for people of different cultural backgrounds.

Red Flag, White Flag

Standard
Employ a wide range of strategies to write and use different writing process elements appropriately to communicate with different audiences for a variety of purposes.

Objective
Students will play a game to practice differentiating fact from opinion.

Materials
fabric or construction paper flags (red and white)

This focus activity will help students differentiate between fact and opinion before they are required to write a research paper (based on fact) or a persuasive essay (based on opinion), a letter to the editor of a periodical publication, and so on.

1. To play the game, give each student a red flag and a white flag. Then ask a question about a book the class is reading, such as: *Who can describe the main character?* Invite a volunteer to describe the character.

2. Tell students to listen carefully. If the student gives an opinion (e.g., *I think the main character is mean*), students raise their red flags. The student then gives evidence from the text (e.g., *He did not feed the hungry kitten, so I think he's mean*). Students then wave their white flags, meaning, *you have proven that your opinion is based on evidence.*

3. Continue asking questions about the text. Students will respond with their red and white flags. Sometimes, a student has an opinion, and there is no evidence to support it. In this case, he or she must persuade the rest of the class to agree. If the student is successful, then white flags are waved.

4. Continue with the activity, asking students to identify both facts and opinions and supply evidence to support them.

Ideas for More Differentiation
Beginning mastery students can work with a partner to discuss whether they should raise a red flag or a white flag.

Extreme Imagery

Strategy
Rehearsal

Standard
Apply knowledge of language structure, language conventions, media techniques, figurative language, and genre to create, critique, and discuss print and nonprint texts.

Objective
Students will write short paragraphs to practice using imagery.

Materials
timer

The root word of *imagery* comes from the Latin word *imitari*, which means "to imitate." What is imagery? Imagery is language that describes something in detail. Imagery uses words that create sensory stimulation; it creates an image in the mind, an imitation of the real thing.

1. Explain to students that using rich, interesting, and specific language makes writing much more interesting. Rich language should paint a picture in the reader's mind, forming a specific image. Imagery is what teacher want when they tell students to show rather than tell in their writing.

2. Define the term *imagery* for students. Then set the timer for five minutes, and demonstrate how to create an extreme image. Write your free flow of ideas on the board while you think aloud. Keep writing until the timer rings. For example, someone who is extremely thirsty: *His tongue feels like a thick, dry washcloth. He feels like a plant whose cells are like dry husks, disintegrating from lack of water. His throat is a hot asphalt road with cars kicking up dust.* Emphasize that similes and metaphors work well for creating imagery.

3. Now tell students it is their opportunity to create an extreme image. Ask: *What can you imagine and then imitate? What words can you choose to form an image in the reader's mind?* Set the timer for five minutes, and tell students to start writing. The following are some ideas from which students can choose:
   - Someone who is extremely tired
   - Someone who is extremely hungry
   - Someone who is extremely angry

- Someone who is extremely embarrassed
- Someone who is extremely excited or happy
- Someone who is extremely sad

4. While students are writing, remind them not to tell why the person is tired or angry, but to create an image of how an extremely tired or angry person looks, acts, or feels. Provide prompts to spark ideas, such as: *You just won the lottery! Describe what "extremely excited" looks like. You lost your new puppy at the park. Describe what "extremely sad" looks like.*

5. When students are finished creating their extreme images, have them exchange papers with a partner. Invite partners to figure out the extreme image being described and then illustrate it. For example, the extreme image is: *I am a block of wood. I don't move except for my knothole eyes that bore through the window, desperately seeking a way out.* The student responds: *You are describing someone who is extremely bored.* Then he or she illustrates the image as it was described.

6. To continually reinforce the concept of imagery, encourage students to look for good examples in stories, articles, and poems they read in and out of class. Tell them to highlight passages that evoke images in their minds. They can copy the text onto a piece of paper or photocopy the passage. Bind together a class collection of powerful images, and allow students to use it as a reference for their own writing.

Ideas for More Differentiation

It is helpful for some students to draw before they write. After providing an extreme prompt, allow these students to make a quick sketch during the timed five minutes. Later, give them another five minutes to write.

Quick Change

Strategies

Role play

Cooperative group
learning

Standard

Apply a wide range of strategies to comprehend, interpret, evaluate, and appreciate texts. Draw on prior experience, interactions with other readers and writers, knowledge of word meaning and of other texts, word identification strategies, and understanding of textual features (e.g., sound-letter correspondence, sentence structure, context, graphics).

Objective

Students will play a game to learn about the elements of a story.

Many students are eager to act for the class. However, some students would rather do anything than perform in front of their classmates! Here is an activity that will give both types of students an opportunity to be involved.

When studying elements (or features) of a story, students learn about plot, point of view, setting, and conflict. Help students gain a deeper understanding of these elements by having them volunteer to role-play for the class, while other students volunteer to be "callers."

1. To begin, remind students about the elements of a story: ***Plot*** *is the overall series of events that drive the story. It can be broken down into introduction, rising action, climax, falling action, and conclusion.* ***Point of view*** *is the identity of the narrative voice, the person or entity through which the reader experiences the story.* ***Setting*** *is the time, place, environment, and surrounding circumstances of a story.* ***Conflict*** *is the struggle a character experiences with nature, another character, society, or him- or herself.*

2. To prepare for the game, divide the class into groups of four. Direct each group to create a list of story elements, referring to books they've read: settings, points of view (characters), plots, and conflicts (e.g., struggle of man against the sea or struggle of a student against a bully).

3. To play the game, choose four callers, and give each caller one of the lists. Callers take turns calling out items from the lists. Invite four volunteer actors to come to the front of the classroom.

4. Provide actors with the first situation, for example: *You are four friends stranded on a deserted island.* (setting) *You want to find a way to get back home.* (plot) *You are fighting against nature, trying to find the best way.* (conflict) Point to an actor. *You are Bill, the main character.* (point of view) *Go!*

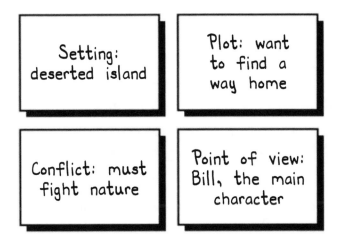

Setting: deserted island

Plot: want to find a way home

Conflict: must fight nature

Point of view: Bill, the main character

5. Have actors role-play the situation. They can try to build a raft, build a fire to catch the attention of passing planes, and so on. Then the first caller says: *Change the setting! You are now lost in a mall! Go!* The actors are now are in a mall, trying to find a way home. Instead of building a raft, they try to get money for bus fare.

6. The next caller says: *Change the plot! You are still in a mall, but your friends dare you to talk like a robot to the sales person.* Actors continue to role-play. Then the third caller says: *Change the conflict! You are now arguing about what is right and wrong. Go!* Actors continue to act according to the new directions. Finally, the fourth caller says: *Change the point of view from Bill to the sales person* (point to a student other than "Bill"). *Go!*

7. After the actors have had a chance to role-play several different scenarios, invite a new group of callers and actors to play the game. Callers can use their lists to help them with ideas for changes. As soon as inspiration hits (and they've given the actors enough time to perform), any caller may request a change.

Ideas for More Differentiation

This game is very engaging but can be complex when all the elements are included. You may want to scaffold the game by changing just one story element per game. For example, just change the setting (an island to a mall to a forest to a phone booth). Then add one more element, such as point of view. As students become proficient, continue to add the remaining elements one by one.

Persuasive Techniques

Standard

Apply knowledge of language structure, language conventions, media techniques, figurative language, and genre to create, critique, and discuss print and nonprint texts.

Objective

Students will identify, analyze, and critique persuasive techniques in the media and then use them in their own writing.

Persuasive techniques are used in literature, speechmaking, and advertising to convince people to agree with a certain idea or point of view. Engage students in a lesson about these techniques.

Glittering Generalities: These are emotionally appealing words associated with highly valued concepts and beliefs. They have positive connotations and conviction but offer no real supporting information. Politicians often use this technique to persuade voters, for example: *I believe in the middle class! I support these great patriots who work hard for their families, providing the food and housing every citizen deserves!*

Flattery: Flattery is excessive or insincere compliments used in order to get something. It is often used in place of real evidence. For example, a person might say to his boss: *Hello, Mr. Jones, you look great! Have you been going to the gym lately? By the way, I really think I should get that promotion!*

Promises: A promise is an assurance that something definitely will or will not be done. One must be careful when using promises in a persuasive piece. For example: *I promise we will never again serve creamed spinach in the cafeteria!* (We'd like to promise, but we really can't.)

Dare: To dare someone is to challenge him or her. For example: *Are you man enough to handle wearing this cologne?*

1. Once students have a good understanding of these persuasive techniques, invite them to bring in examples from magazine and newspaper ads or illustrate a television commercial. Display the ads on a bulletin board titled *Gotcha! We Can't Be Persuaded!* Then invite students to label the persuasive techniques used.

2. Invite students to complete a project of their choice based on the techniques they've learned:
   - Students can create a commercial. Have them bring in something from home that no one would ever really want, such as an old sock or a piece of chewed gum. Their job is to persuade the audience to buy it using one or all of the persuasive techniques. Ask the audience to identify which techniques were used.
   - If it is an election year, videotape different candidates' speeches, and allow students to watch and analyze them to determine which persuasive techniques are used. If students are having a school or class election, candidates may write speeches to persuade their classmates to vote for them.
   - Students can integrate persuasive writing in their study of social studies. Perhaps they can take a stance on the Revolutionary War by deciding whether they will remain loyal to or rebel against King George.
   - To augment their study of current events and community issues, students can write persuasive letters to the city council or newspaper editor.

3. Remind students to do the following when developing their persuasive arguments:
   - Provide an introduction that grabs the audience's attention.
   - Establish facts that support an argument.
   - Clarify values that are relevant to the audience.
   - Sequence facts and values in order of importance to build the argument.
   - Form and state the conclusion.
   - Persuade the audience that the conclusion is based on agreed-upon facts and values.

Ideas for More Differentiation

Breaking the writing process into steps will be helpful for even your most skilled writers. Brainstorm during the prewriting process to develop both sides of the argument. Break the drafting step into several stages (introduction, body, conclusion). Students can peer-edit each other's writing, if needed.

Wonderful Words

Standard

Apply a wide range of strategies to comprehend, interpret, evaluate, and appreciate texts. Draw on prior experience, interactions with other readers and writers, knowledge of word meaning and of other texts, word identification strategies, and understanding of textual features (e.g., sound-letter correspondence, sentence structure, context, graphics).

Objective

Students will learn about the origins of English words and use a dictionary to find word origins.

Materials

Word Origins reproducible
dictionaries

The English language developed from many different sources. People created words; words were borrowed from other languages; and words developed over the centuries from ancestral languages. Invite students into the exciting world of etymology with this word discovery activity.

1. Explain to students that people often create new words from base words. Adding *er* or *ing* to a base word can create a new noun, verb, or gerund (e.g., *teach, teacher, teaching*). Nouns can also be changed to abbreviations and then to verbs (e.g., *instant message, IM, IMing*).

2. Provide some background information about the origins of words. Explain that understanding word origins is key to increased reading comprehension and vocabulary development. It can also help them to identify and decipher unknown words.
   - The English language derives from one single language called *Proto-Germanic*.
   - Dialects emerged as people moved away from each other. This mother language developed into other sister languages. Words changed over the centuries, but the core English words used today developed from the Proto-Germanic language after going through the stages of Old English, Middle English, and Modern English.
   - Thousands of base words have been borrowed from other languages. As English-speaking people made contact with the rest of the world, the English language became infused with

words from Latin, Greek, Italian, Arabic, French, Norwegian, and many other languages. For example, *spaghetti* and *piano* are Italian words, and *aerosol* and *monopoly* derive from Greek roots.

3. Invite students to explore word origins using the dictionary. A good dictionary explains the symbols used in its definitions. For example, in *Webster's New World Dictionary*, the first few pages include a guide for using the dictionary. Invite students to turn to this section as you review it. This guide explains symbols such as <, which means "derived from." The dictionary also includes a list of abbreviations, such as *OL*, which means "Old Latin."

4. Give students a copy of the **Word Origins reproducible (page 74)**. Instruct ▶ them to use this sheet to explore the origins and meanings of words. Students will record the modern definition, the origin, and the meaning of the original word.

5. Encourage students to keep a running list of words and their origins throughout the year and to add more sheets as needed. These sheets are great for review or studying for a test!

Word Origins Page 74

Ideas for More Differentiation

- Students could also use alternate resources to discover word origins. Encourage them to use the Internet, interview university professors, or check out books from the library.

- For beginning mastery students, provide a prepared list of words to research. As students develop their skills, encourage them to find word origins for words they are curious about. Encourage students with a high degree of mastery to extend their lists with information about the context of the words (i.e., why they evolved).

Name _____   Date _____

Word Origins

Directions: Use the dictionary to research words. Find the modern definition, the origin, and the meaning of the origin.

Word	Modern Definition	Origin	Word/Meaning
constitution	document containing government laws	Old French	constituer/ to set up

978-1-4129-5341-2 • © Corwin Press

Found Poetry

Standard
Employ a wide range of strategies while writing, and use different writing process elements appropriately to communicate with different audiences for a variety of purposes.

Strategy
Presentation

Objective
Students will use different kinds of text to create poetry and then present their poems to the class.

Some students may be reluctant to write poetry. A nonthreatening way to engage students is to have them create found poetry.

1. Explain to students that *found poetry* is created using words, phrases, or sentences from existing text. It can come from a newspaper article, a textbook, or even a shampoo bottle.

2. Invite students to bring in something with text on it, such as an empty cereal box or magazine article. They will select words or phrases and arrange them on a page. They may alter punctuation and capitalization, but they cannot add any words.

3. As students are creating their found poems, remind them that their poem may or may not convey the same meaning as the original text.

   Here is a found poem created from a fifth grade social studies text (conveys the same meaning):
   > *Special gatherings*
   > *Celebrations*
   > *Potlaches!*
   > *Some members of*
   > *Some clans*
   > *Spent years*
   > *Preparing hundreds of gifts to be given away at Potlaches—to show off the things they owned!*

   Here is a found poem from a shampoo bottle (does not convey the same meaning):
   > *Fine...*
   > *Fly away*
   > *If it makes you stronger*
   > *Work!*
   > *A little goes a long way*
   > *When you need to feel*
   > *Hold on, make this a habit*
   > *A little goes a long way.*

4. Invite students to think of an interesting or dramatic way to present their poems to the class. Encourage them to use illustrations, other visuals, or music. Provide class time for each student to give his or her presentation.

Strategy Cube

Standard

Apply knowledge of language structure, language conventions, media techniques, figurative language, and genre to create, critique, and discuss print and nonprint texts.

Objective

Students will respond to prompts about text using a strategy cube.

Materials

Strategy Cube reproducible

scissors

tape

Focus activities help to open students' mental files, preparing them for upcoming lessons. Use a strategy cube to engage students in a quick cubing activity that allows them to hone their reading comprehension skills.

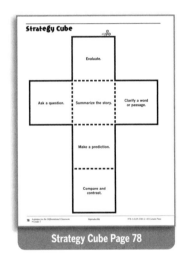

Strategy Cube Page 78

1. Reproduce, cut out, and assemble the **Strategy Cube (page 78)**. You may find it best to form a sturdier cube by printing the page on heavy paper or even cardstock. On the cube are the following strategies for improving reading comprehension:

    Summarize the story.

    Clarify a word or passage.

    Ask a question.

    Make a prediction.

    Compare and contrast.

    Evaluate.

2. Before presenting a reading lesson or to review concepts, toss the cube to a student. Have the student roll the cube on his or her desk. Provide a passage or text element for the student to work with. For example, if a student rolls *Clarify a word or passage,* provide a word or passage from a current reading assignment. If a student rolls *Compare and contrast,* give the student two characters, two story events, or two different stories to compare and contrast.

3. Have the student record the directive from the cube and the passage you provided before tossing the cube back to you or to another student. Provide another passage or story element for the next student.

4. Continue tossing the cube until all students have a directive and a passage.

5. Allow adequate time for students to apply their cube directive to the passage you provided. When time is up, invite students to share their work with small groups or the whole class.

Ideas for More Differentiation

Students can create their own cubes with directives that apply to the information they want to review. Invite them to tape their cubes together and use them to review material in small groups.

Strategy Cube

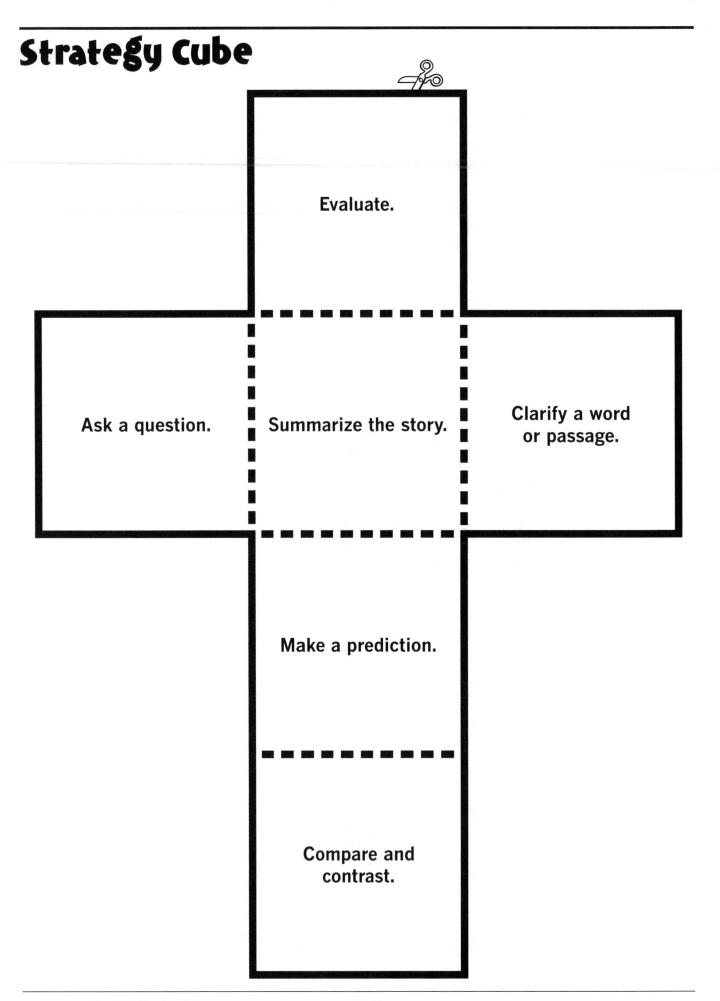

Evaluate.

Ask a question.

Summarize the story.

Clarify a word or passage.

Make a prediction.

Compare and contrast.

Reproducible

Main Idea, Details, GO!

Standard
Apply knowledge of language structure, language conventions, media techniques, figurative language, and genre to create, critique, and discuss print and nonprint texts.

Objective
Students will respond to prompts by providing details to support main ideas from their reading.

Materials
squishy ball

Strategy
Focus activity

This focus activity is great for review in any of the content areas and can also be used as a precomposing step in the writing process. It helps students learn the structure of a paragraph with main ideas and supporting details.

1. Begin by making a written or mental list of information you want students to review. Have students stand at their desks or in a large circle. State a main idea sentence to the class. For example, if students are reading Elizabeth Winthrop's *The Castle in the Attic,* you might say: *Mrs. Phillips was wise to read* King Arthur and the Knights of the Round Table *to William.*

2. Toss the squishy ball to a student, and say: *GO!* That student must give a detail that proves the main idea. For example: *William was able to speak to the Silver Knight in the same formal language.* That student then tosses the squishy ball to another student, who must give another detail that supports the main idea.

3. When you say: *Done,* the last student with the ball tosses it back to you.

4. As students continue to provide details, restate the main idea. Encourage them to use details in complete sentences as they would when writing a paragraph. Soon, the verbal paragraph emerges!

5. When you've gathered enough supporting details, invite students to help you write the paragraph on the board.

Ideas for More Differentiation
Some students may find it helpful to see the main idea sentence written on the board for visual reference.

CHAPTER 5

Physical Education, Art, and Music

Bowling for Homework Passes

Objective
Students will learn accurate throwing skills while bowling with water bottles.

Materials
sets of ten 1-liter water bottles (1/3 full of water)
tennis balls
masking tape or sidewalk chalk
index cards (scorecards)

1. Divide the class into teams of three. One team member is the bowler, one is the pinsetter/ball fetcher, and one is the scorekeeper. The object of the game is to knock down the water bottles with the tennis ball. Each player gets three chances per turn to throw the ball and earns one point for each bottle knocked over.

2. On the blacktop, mark bowling lanes with chalk or tape (two long parallel lines for each team). Set up water bottles in a triangular shape as you would set up bowling pins: one row of four, one row of three, one row of two, and a single bottle in front.

3. To play the game, the bowler gets three chances to roll the ball down the lane to knock down the water bottles, or "pins." The pinsetter tells the scorekeeper how many pins were knocked down. The pinsetter then sets up the pins for the scorekeeper, who then becomes the bowler. The bowler becomes the pinsetter, and the pinsetter becomes the scorekeeper.

4. Students may play against each other or another team. The player or team with the most points after a set number of turns per player wins. Instead of bowling for dollars or stickers, students can bowl for homework passes!

Ideas for More Differentiation
Depending upon the strength of students' bowling arms, you may shorten or lengthen the alleys. Try to group more athletic students with less skilled players to ensure the teams are balanced.

Harry Potter Hockey

Objective

Students will play a hockey-type game using brooms, wastebaskets, and paper balls.

Strategy
Game

Materials

2 brooms
2 rectangular wastebaskets
ball of newspaper wrapped in duct tape

Tie this interactive game into students' love of the Harry Potter books. In these stories, the students play a game with broomsticks. Invite students to give this game a fun name similar to the one used in the Harry Potter series.

1. Have students line up opposite each other in two lines (the sidelines of a basketball court work very well). Place the wastebaskets on their sides between the two lines, one at the beginning and one at the middle.

2. Assign each player a number. When assigning numbers, give equally skilled students the same number (i.e., give a pair of athletic students the same numbers and a pair of less athletic students the same numbers). This way, students will be more equally matched for competition.

3. Place two broomsticks and the newspaper ball in the middle of the court. The object of the game is for students to earn points by sweeping the ball into a wastebasket.

4. Call a number. The student from each team with that number grabs a broom and tries to sweep the ball into a wastebasket. Teammates may help by kicking the ball if it comes close to the line, but they can't move from the line. Points are earned by getting the ball into a wastebasket.

5. To make the game more challenging, a student may earn an extra point if after sweeping the ball into a wastebasket, he or she takes it out and tosses it to a teammate. That student then tries to make a free throw into the basketball hoop.

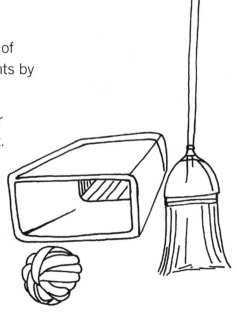

Laundry Day

Objective
Students will participate in a relay race.

Materials
3 laundry baskets
basket of rags
9 cones or markers

The Presidential Fitness Challenge includes a test called the Shuttle Run, which measures speed and agility. This game is similar to the Shuttle Run, but it is a lot more fun!

1. To play the game, divide the class into three teams. Place three cones on the grass or blacktop in a line, 15 feet apart. Create two more lines, leaving ten feet between each line. At the first cone, place an empty laundry basket. Divide the rags into two equal piles, and place one pile at each of the remaining cones. Each team lines up behind the laundry basket. See the diagram below:

			Rags		Rags
Basket	A	....	B	....	C
			Rags		Rags
Basket	A	....	B	....	C
			Rags		Rags
Basket	A	....	B	....	C

2. To begin, Player 1 in each line grabs the basket and runs from point A to point B. He or she puts the rags in the basket, runs back to point A, and dumps them. Player 1 then runs to point C, puts the rags in the basket, runs back and dumps them.

3. Player 2 must put half the rags back into the basket, run to point B, and dump them out. He or she then runs back to point A, puts the rest of the rags in the basket, dumps them at point C, and runs back to point A with the empty basket.

4. Player 3 repeats what Player 1 did, Player 4 repeats what Player 2 did, and so on, until all players have participated. The team that finishes first is the winner of Laundry Day!

Ideas for More Differentiation
Have students complete the game at an increasingly faster rate. Use a stopwatch to time each student and get baseline data. After playing for several weeks, test students again to measure their improvement.

Fitness Frisbee

Objective
Partners will participate in events from the Presidential Fitness Challenge.

Strategy
Rehearsal

Materials
Frisbees® (1 for every 2 students)
access to a bar for chin-ups

This fitness activity builds cardiovascular and muscle strength.

1. Take students out into an open area, such as the playground or a sports field. Divide the class into pairs, and give each pair a Frisbee®.

2. To play the game, have partners scatter across the open field. Partner A begins by throwing a Frisbee® to Partner B. Partner B catches the Frisbee®, while Partner A runs to him or her. Then they take turns holding each other's feet while each does ten **sit-ups**.

3. Then Partner B runs away as Partner A throws the Frisbee® to him or her. While Partner B catches it, Partner B joins Partner A. Then they both do as many **push-ups** as they can. Have partners continue throwing the Frisbee® to one another and meeting to perform another fitness exercise, such as **sit-and-reach** and **pull-ups.**

    Sit-and-Reach Students sit with their legs out in front like a V, toes pointing upward. They grasp their thumbs and gently reach forward as far as they can, with palms facing downward. Tell students to stretch slowly three times without bouncing.

    Pull-ups Students hang from a bar. Remind them not to kick their feet. Tell them to pull up as smoothly as possible as many times as possible and then drop down.

4. After students have cycled through the routine several times, eward them for all their hard work by allowing them to play with the Frisbees®.

Ideas for More Differentiation
Before beginning the activity, show students how to do individual exercises (sit-ups, push-ups, sit-and-reach, and pull-ups), as well as how to throw a Frisbee®.

Still Life of Personal Artifacts

Strategy
Multiple intelligences

Objective

Students will create a still life of personal artifacts.

Materials

student artifacts from Personal Artifacts activity (see page 40)
hand towels or linen napkins
drawing paper
fine-line black markers
crayons, oil pastels, tempera paint
still-life examples

1. Describe the concept of a still life to students. Show several examples from books or the Internet. Explain that a still life can consist of a basket of fruit, a vase of flowers, or any arrangement of commonplace, nonmoving objects.

2. Direct students to arrange their personal artifacts on their desks or in an art center. Each student will need some fabric, such as a hand towel or a linen napkin, to drape around the arrangement. Have students place artifacts at different levels, especially if they are similar in size. (Students may need to place artifacts on a book or small box.) Help students arrange their artifacts asymmetrically to make the display as interesting as possible.

3. Have students choose the point of view, or perspective, from which they will draw. Perhaps they want to sit on the floor and look upward or sit to the side. Suggest that students start drawing with the middle object; then they can draw to the right of it, above it, to the left of it, and below it.

4. Direct students to begin with a light sketch to create the overall composition. Then they can go back and draw contour lines, which follow the objects' shapes. Make sure they include shading by using the side of the pencil and create texture and patterns using thick, thin, short, long, curved, or straight lines.

5. When drawings are finished, students may choose to trace the pencil lines with fine-line black marker. They can then color in the drawing using oil pastels, crayons, or tempera paint.

Ideas for More Differentiation

Some students may have difficulty drawing the entire compostion at once. Have these students focus on and draw one object at a time.

Portrait of an Artist, a President, or a Fifth Grader

Objective
Students will create a portrait using collage techniques.

Strategy
Center activity

Materials
tag board
collage materials (paper and fabric scraps, magazine cutouts, foil, waxed paper)
art supplies

The word *portrait* conjures images of George Washington, Vincent Van Gogh, and even 8" x 10" school pictures. This center allows students to take a creative, personalized approach to creating a portrait.

1. Invite students to explore which portrait they would like to create. They can research ideas on the Internet using the key words *famous portraits*. Many Web sites show portraits of celebrities, babies, and historical figures.

2. Tell students that they will create a portrait using a variety of art supplies and a collage technique. After they have chosen their subject, they must consider composition. There are a variety of elements to consider:
   - different shapes in the portrait (ovals, circles, rectangles)
   - positive and negative space (positive space is the subject; negative space is the area around the subject)
   - color contrast (primary, secondary, and tertiary colors)
   - balance of pattern (it is useful to repeat a pattern, color, and/ or shape to create unity in the design, but repeat it an odd number of times, and change it slightly for variety)

3. Students do not have to use the same colors as in the original portrait (if they want a purple princess, so be it!). They will use a cut-and-paste collage technique to create their portraits. They can draw the piece they want to cut out or use random, ripped shapes or magazine cutouts that relate to the subject. Encourage students to configure their design before they glue it down so they can move things around or change them as needed.

Stuck on Symbols

Objective

Students will choose an American symbol to represent in a glue-line relief print.

Materials

white crayon or chalk
10" x 16" smooth cardboard pieces
white glue in plastic bottles with nozzles
water soluble black ink
large Styrofoam meat trays (inking pads)
soft rubber brayers
colored tissue paper or plain newsprint
12" x 18" colorful construction paper
aprons or old T-shirts

1. Brainstorm with students a list of American symbols, such as the flag, the Statue of Liberty, the Liberty Bell, Uncle Sam, and the bald eagle. Ask students to use their creativity and personal feelings about America to think of the symbols most meaningful to them. Encourage them to think beyond traditional symbols and also imagine those that are nontraditional. Then have them find pictures of these symbols in books or on the Internet to use as references for the project.

2. Tell students they will create a print of their symbol by creating a glue-line stamp. First, have them use white crayon or chalk to draw a simple pattern of their symbol on a piece of cardboard. White will stand out against the brown background. Have students trace the lines carefully with glue. (Remind them to squeeze the glue bottles gently to create lines, not blobs, of glue.) Allow the glue drawings to dry overnight.

3. When glue drawings are completely dry, ask students to put on aprons or old T-shirts to protect their clothing.

4. Have students go to the inking center, which is liberally covered with newspaper. Tell them to squeeze some ink onto the inking pad and then roll the brayer in it until it is tacky.

5. Have students roll the inked brayer over their glue-line drawing until it is completely covered. Have them place a sheet of tissue paper or newsprint on top of their inked drawing, and press down gently, beginning in the center and then spreading outward.

(Remind them not to press too hard or they will pick up more than just the raised glue-line stamp.)

6. Have students carefully lift off the print and place it on a sheet of newspaper to dry. Allow at least the full morning or afternoon for prints to dry. Then help students mount their prints on large sheets of colorful construction paper to create frames.

Ideas for More Differentiation

Encourage students to write acrostic poems to accompany their symbol prints. For example:

Freedom
Land of the brave
America
Government by the people, for the people

Starry Nights

Strategies

Structured center

Journaling

Objective

Students will study Vincent Van Gogh's painting *The Starry Night*, and then recreate it using similar painting techniques.

Materials

large print of Van Gogh's *The Starry Night*
tempera paint
paper plates
paintbrushes
12" x 18" painting paper
oil pastels
bowls of water
recording of "Vincent (Starry, Starry Night)" by Don McLean
CD or cassette player

Introduce students to the fascinating world of Vincent Van Gogh's art through this stimulating, thought-provoking activity.

1. Display a print of Van Gogh's *The Starry Night,* and then give students some background information:

   Van Gogh's *The Starry Night,* painted in 1889, is one of the world's most well-known images. In his painting, Van Gogh heavily used the element of line. Curved lines in the sky and swirling clouds create a sense of motion in a still scene; the eye moves to connect the dots between glowing stars. A peaceful town lies below; the church steeple seems to watch over the town. In the foreground there is a dark, wavy image, which most people agree is a cyprus tree.

   Van Gogh used a technique called *impaste,* which means he covered the canvas thickly with paint. He used short brushstrokes and even squeezed paint from the tube directly onto the canvas. Students will imitate this short brushstroke in their paintings.

2. Bring students to the art center for the first session. They will use oil pastels to sketch the cyprus tree, the stars, the church steeple, and several town buildings seen in *The Starry Night.* They will also use yellow pastel to draw short, moving lines that look like paths of light in the sky.

3. For the second session, students will use a paper plate to create a paint palette. Have them put blobs of red, blue, and yellow paint

around the edge of the plate. Then have them mix primary colors to create secondary colors (purple, green, orange). Students will also need a plate with just white paint and black paint to make lighter and darker colors (tints and shades).

4. Invite students to begin painting. Using a wide paintbrush, have them lay on tempera paint thickly in short, curving strokes to paint the sky, tree, and starlight. They will use smaller brushes to paint the town buildings. Encourage students to take their time; this step may take more than one session. Many students will try to copy Van Gogh's color palette, which is great! However, encourage students to create their own color palette if they wish. Allow them to put their personalities into their versions of *The Starry Night*.

5. While students are painting, play Don McLean's popular song "Vincent (Starry, Starry Night)." This song is about Van Gogh's tragedy. Van Gogh felt misunderstood and eventually ended his life, partly because he was unsuccessful as an artist in his time. It is now thought that he suffered from bipolar disorder.

    Van Gogh wrote: *I don't care much whether I live a longer or shorter time... The world concerns me only insofar as I feel a certain indebtedness and duty toward it because I have walked this earth for thirty years, and, out of gratitude, want to leave some souvenir in the shape of drawings or pictures—not made to please a certain taste in art, but to express a sincere human feeling.*

6. Ask students to reflect on which human feelings Van Gogh was trying to convey in *The Starry Night*. Ask them to reflect on their own feelings while looking at this painting. Ask: *How do Van Gogh's brushstroke techniques and use of color influence your opinion?*

7. Ask students to continue to reflect on this painting in their journals. Have them also write how they felt recreating their own version of *The Starry Night*.

Yankee Doodle and More

Objective

Students will research American period music and write their own song lyrics.

An important element of studying American history is studying period music. During the colonial period, the first settlers brought along their music and instruments; they brought hymns as well as fiddles, guitars, viols, and flutes. As time passed, an American style of music developed, influenced by Native American music, African music, European classical music, and the improvisations and techniques of self-taught American musicians.

It is surprisingly easy to research period music. For example, if you use the key words *colonial music* while searching on the Internet, you will find many Web sites that offer tunes from colonial times. You can buy songbooks and CDs, and some Web sites allow you to listen to songs. Try the McNeil Music Web site at: *www.mcneilmusic.com*, which allows you to listen to several songs and provides a historical explanation of the music.

1. Invite students to research period music, including the meanings of songs they know, such as "Yankee Doodle." A British man wrote the lyrics to make fun of the raggedy colonial soldiers. Encourage students to study African American spirituals during the Civil War period. Some slave songs were actually directions for runaway slaves escaping through the Underground Railroad. "Wade in the Water" and "Follow the Drinking Gourd" are two famous examples of such coded songs.

2. Have students segue from researching existing songs to writing their own lyrics (and melodies, if they are able) about a specific time period, perhaps one they are currently studying (e.g., the Louisiana Purchase or the Lewis and Clark expedition). Ask students if they can think of lyrics to inspire key characters in the event or enrich their own understanding.

3. As students write, introduce the term *disambiguation*, which means "call and response." It is a musical technique that Africans brought with them to America. It is used in jazz, blues, folk music, and more. One instrument plays a melody and another instrument copies it. It is similar to echoing when singing songs. Invite students to consider using call-and-response when writing their lyrics.

The following example is about the Lewis and Clark expedition:

Meriwether Lewis was a pathfinder.
A pathfinder?
Yes, a pathfinder.
He found his way through an unknown region.
An unknown region?
Yes, an unknown region, the Louisiana Purchase.
Lewis and Clark, that's William Clark, a cartographer.
A cartographer?
Yes, a mapmaker; they formed a group
Called the Corps of Discovery.
Corps of Discovery?
Yes, Discovery.
They met a woman named Sacagawea.
Sacagawea?
Yes, Sacagawea, who spoke the Shoshone language.
She translated for Lewis and Clark.
She translated?
Yes, translated, and together they reached the Pacific Ocean.
The Pacific Ocean?
Yes!

4. Students can perform their lyrics using a drum or other simple classroom instruments as accompaniment. Have them choose a group of students to chant the lead part and another group to chant the echo.

978-1-4129-5341-2

Music in Our Lives

Objective

Students will keep a log of their interaction with music for one day.

Materials

Music in My Life Log reproducible

Music augments every aspect of our daily lives. Even people who don't listen to music often experience it through commercial jingles, holiday songs, and even singing in the shower!

1. Engage students in a discussion about music in their daily lives. Explain that the advent of electricity (radio, television) made music accessible to everyone. Listening to music became as easy as turning a switch. Prior to the 20th century, if people wanted to hear music, they had to play an instrument or go to a concert to hear the town band.

2. Point out that people use music in a variety of ways. They listen to it while exercising or to help them relax. People listen to music while they dance, sing, wash dishes, drive cars, do homework, and cook dinner. Advertisers use music to sell products. Music itself is a product; it is bought and sold in stores and over the Internet.

3. Give students a copy of the **Music in My Life Log (page 93)**. Ask them to chart their interactions with music for one day. (You should complete one as well!) Point out the section that notes the appropriateness of certain songs for certain places or activities. Ask students: *What makes one song better for a certain activity and place than another song? Why?* Encourage students to use specific words to describe music, such as *rhythm, beat, melody, instrumental,* and *vocal.*

4. Invite students to share their completed music logs with the class. Use the information to create a class graph that shows data such as the most popular song, artist, or activity to do with music. Make sure to share your music log as well. Discussing music and the way it affects lives will bond your classroom community!

Music in My Life Log Page 93

Music in My Life Log

Directions: As you go through your day, notice all the music you hear. Fill out this form to keep track of the role music plays in your life!

1. Type of Music	2. Type of Music	3. Type of Music
Time of Day	Time of Day	Time of Day
Where are you?	Where are you?	Where are you?
What are you doing?	What are you doing?	What are you doing?
Is the music appropriate? Explain:	Is the music appropriate? Explain:	Is the music appropriate? Explain:
What mood does the music create?	What mood does the music create?	What mood does the music create?

What's the Dressing?

Strategies

Analogy

Sponge activities

Objective

Students will learn songs to help build a common cultural foundation.

Ask students if they have ever heard of America described as a melting pot where people of all cultures melt together to create that uniquely American flavor. Explain that the term *melting pot* was then changed to *salad bowl* to demonstrate the need for different cultures to combine together as a unit but keep their separate identities. If America is indeed a salad bowl, what is the "dressing" that keeps us together? What common foundation helps us grow together as a country, even while keeping our separate cultural identities?

Guide students to see that music can be the dressing for American culture! In the past, nursery rhymes were the backbone of childhood music and chants. Most children could recite them, even if they didn't understand them. Today, students are familiar with all different kinds of music due to advanced technology, such as MP3 players, iPods, CDs, and computer downloads.

Include music in simple sponge activities to fill in those extra minutes in the classroom. Don't just play the music; provide the lyrics so students can sing along. Do some research and find out who wrote particular songs and why. Talk to your fellow teachers and parent helpers. What songs and pieces of music provide that common cultural foundation, or dressing for the salad? Some examples include: "Somewhere Over the Rainbow," Brahms' "Lullaby," Vivalid's "Four Seasons," Pachelbel's "Canon," "I've Been Working on the Railroad," "The Yankee Doodle Boy," "America the Beautiful," "You'll Never Walk Alone," "The Impossible Dream," "Comin' Round the Mountain," "White Christmas," "When the Saints Go Marching In," and "Take Me Out to the Ball Game."

Invite students to bring in songs from home. They can ask their parents about songs they remember from their childhood or bring in songs that are meaningful for them or their families. Encourage students to bring in songs that represent their culture or ancestry in some way.

Fifth Grade Foley Artists

Objective

Students will create sound effects to accompany readings of selected passages.

Strategy
Cooperative group learning

Materials

found materials to create sound effects
text to read for performance

Introduce students to the fascinating world of the Foley artist. This project allows all of your students to become Foley artists right in the classroom!

1. Explain to students that a Foley artist is the person who creates and records sound effects for movies and commercials. The Foley artist gets his or her title from Jack Foley, one of the original practitioners of sound effects. For the sound of two people fighting, the Foley artist might thump watermelons together and break celery (to make the sound of bones breaking).

2. Invite students to become Foley artists for a day. Place students in cooperative groups to create their own sound effects for a dramatic reading. First, ask them to work together to choose a passage for their reading. Perhaps they want to read an exciting passage from their current literature book or a passage from their social studies text about Native Americans.

3. After students select a passage, they will need time to find materials that make the desired sound effects. The can use background music, as well. Create a center where students can choose from a variety of materials such as foil, paper, paper bags, cookie sheets, combs, marbles, and classical music and jazz CDs. Encourage students to think creatively!

4. Finally, invite each group to perform their reading for the class. Make sure they have plenty of time to practice reading and timing their sound effects ahead of time. Ask the class to vote on their favorite presentations or those with the most effective or creative sound effects.

Ideas for More Differentiation

Students can record their oral readings and sound effects and place them in a listening center for others to enjoy.

References

Anglik.net: The Online Resource for Students of English as a Second Language or Foreign Language. (n.d). *A brief history of the English language.* Retrieved September 28, 2006, from http://www.anglik.net/englishlanguagehistory. htm.

Ben's Guide to U.S. government for Kids. (n.d). *Songs and oaths: Yankee Doodle.* Retrieved November 6, 2006, from http://bensguide.gpo. gove/3-5/symbols/yankee.html.

Famous Quotes and Famous Sayings. (n.d). *Famous quotes.* (1993—2007). Retrieved September 9, 2006, from http://quotations.home. worldnet.att.net.

Fat Calories.com. (n.d). *The fast food nutrition explorer.* Retrieved September 1, 2006, from http://www.fatcalories.com.

FilmSound.org. (n.d). *Foley artistry: The story of Jack Foley.* Retrieved November 6, 2006, from http://www.filmsound.org/foley.

Fittante, A., RD, MS, CDE. *BD Getting started™: Fast food guide.* Retrieved September 1, 2006, from http://www.bddiabetes.com./us/download/13A_fastfoodguide.pdf.

General Mills. (2006). *General Mills: History of innovation.* Retrieved September 10, 2006, from www. generalmills.com/corporate/company/history.aspx.

Gregory, G. H., & Chapman, C. (2002). *Differentiated instructional strategies: One size doesn't fit all (2nd ed.).* Thousand Oaks, CA: Corwin Press.

Harcourt Brace social studies fifth grade. (2000). Orlando, Atlanta, Austin, Boston, San Francisco, Chicago, Dallas, New York, Toronto, London: Harcourt Brace & Company.

Harcourt science fifth grade. (2000). Orlando, FL: Harcourt School Publishers.

McNeil Music, Inc. (n.d.). *Colonial and revolution songs.* Retrieved November 6, 2006, from http://www.mcneilmusic.com/rev.html.

Moonlight Systems. *Lyrics to popular moon songs.* Retrieved November 10, 2006, from http://moonlightsys.com/themoon/lyrics.html.

National Council for the Social Studies. (2002). *Expectations of excellence: Curriculum standards for social studies.* Silver Spring, MD: National Council for the Social Studies (NCSS).

National Council of Teachers of English and International Reading Association. (1996). *Standards for the English language arts.* Urbana, IL: National Council of Teachers of English (NCTE).

National Council of Teachers of Mathematics. (2005). *Principles and standards for school mathematics.* Reston, VA: National Council of Teachers of Mathematics (NCTM).

National Research Council. (2005). *National science education standards.* Washington, DC: National Academy Press.

New Jersey State Museum Planetarium & Raritan Valley Community College Planetarium. (n.d.). *Educator's guide to… "follow the drinking gourd" (part 1).* Retrieved November 10, 2006, from the Madison Metro. School District Web site: http://www.madison.k12.wi.us/planetarium/ftdg1.htm.

The President's Challenge.org. (n.d). *Physical fitness test.* Retrieved October 1, 2006, from http://www.presidentschallenge.org/educators/program_details/physical_fitness_test.aspx.

Radiochemistry Society (Los Alamos National Laboratory). (n.d.). *Periodic table of the elements.* Retrieved September 6, 2006, from http//www.radiochemistry.org.

WebExhibits.com. (n.d.). *Van Gogh's letters: Unabridged and annotated: Letter from Vincent Van Gogh to Theo van Gogh, The Hauge, c 4–8 August 1883.* Retrieved November 6, 2006, from http://webexhibits.org/vangogh/letter/12/309.htm.

Wikipedia: The free encyclopedia. Retrieved November 10, 2006, from http://en.wikipedia.org/wiki.